A Flavour of Liberty

BCHA

Published by New Generation Publishing in 2024

Copyright © Poppy Blundell 2024

First Edition

The author asserts the moral right under the Copyright, Designs and Patents Act 1988 to be identified as the author of this work.

All Rights reserved. No part of this publication may be reproduced, stored in a retrieval system or transmitted, in any form or by any means without the prior consent of the author, nor be otherwise circulated in any form of binding or cover other than that which it is published and without a similar condition being imposed on the subsequent purchaser.

ISBN: 978-1-83563-399-1

www.newgeneration-publishing.com

New Generation Publishing

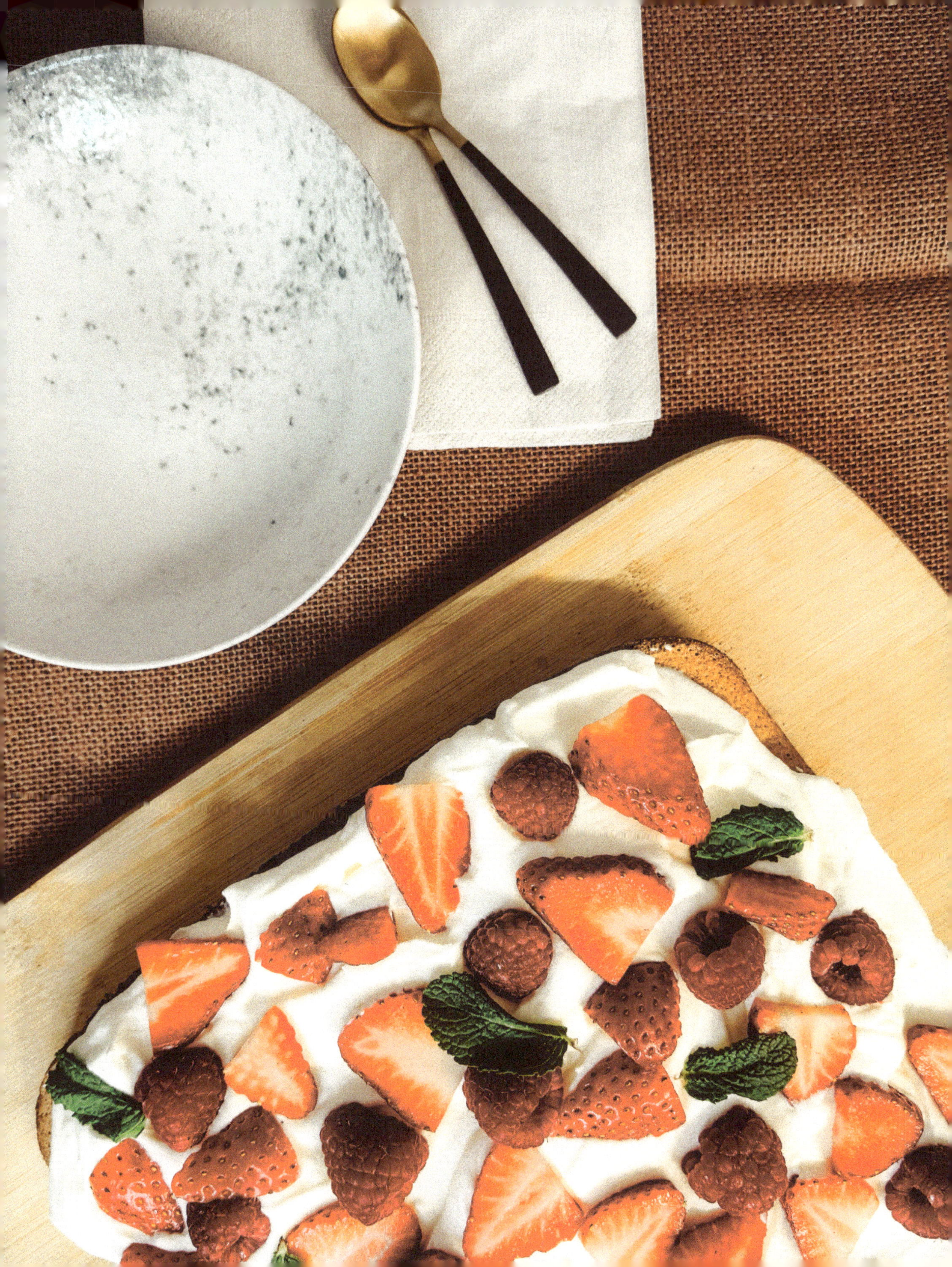

This book is dedicated to all survivors of modern slavery,
and to all those who are still enslaved.

One person at a time is how we end slavery.
Never underestimate the power of raising awareness.

Contents

- Modern Slavery Facts and Figures — vi
- The Liberty Project — vii
- A Flavour of Liberty — viii
- Mains — 1
    a. Albanian Tave Kosi – Lamb Yoghurt Dinner
    b. Albanian Tave Pulu – The Chicken Dish
    c. Bangladesh Chicken Curry
    d. Chinese Stir Fry Beef
    e. English Beef Pie
    f. Indian Sag Paneer – Cheese Curry
    g. Italian Chilli Prawn Linguine
    h. Malawian Ndiwo and Nsima – Relish Vegetables and corn meal
    i. Nigerian Egusi Soup and Fufu
    j. Pakistani Aloo Tikka
    k. Romanian Cabbage Rolls
    l. South African Sweet Potato Hot Pot
    m. Zimbabwean Stir Fry Beef
- Side Dishes — 33
    a. English Cheesy Mash
    b. Mexican Potato Wedges
    c. Thai Roasted Vegetable
    d. Zimbabwean Peanut Butter Rices
- Deserts — 39
    a. Albanian Shendetlie – Honey Cake
    b. Albanian Tres Leches – Milk Cake
    c. American Worms in Mud – Oreo Cheesecake
    d. Brazilian Sweet Rice
- Sponsors — 50
- Thank You — 51
- BCHA — 52

Modern Slavery Facts and Figures

Modern slavery is happening all around us. People you walk past in the streets, in shops or on building sites, could be living and working in horrendous conditions, held against their will with violence or being exploited.

The Shocking Reality:
- **Almost 50 million people** globally are estimated to live in modern slavery, according to the International Labour Organisation. The true number is likely to be much higher due to the hidden nature of this crime.
- In 2023, 44% of survivors claimed to have been exploited when they were children.
- **99% of survivors** are never rescued.

A Glimpse into the UK:
In 2023, 17,004 potential survivors of modern slavery were referred into the National Referral Mechanism (NRM). This is the UK's framework for supporting potential survivors of modern-day slavery. For adult survivors, 76% were male and 24% were female.

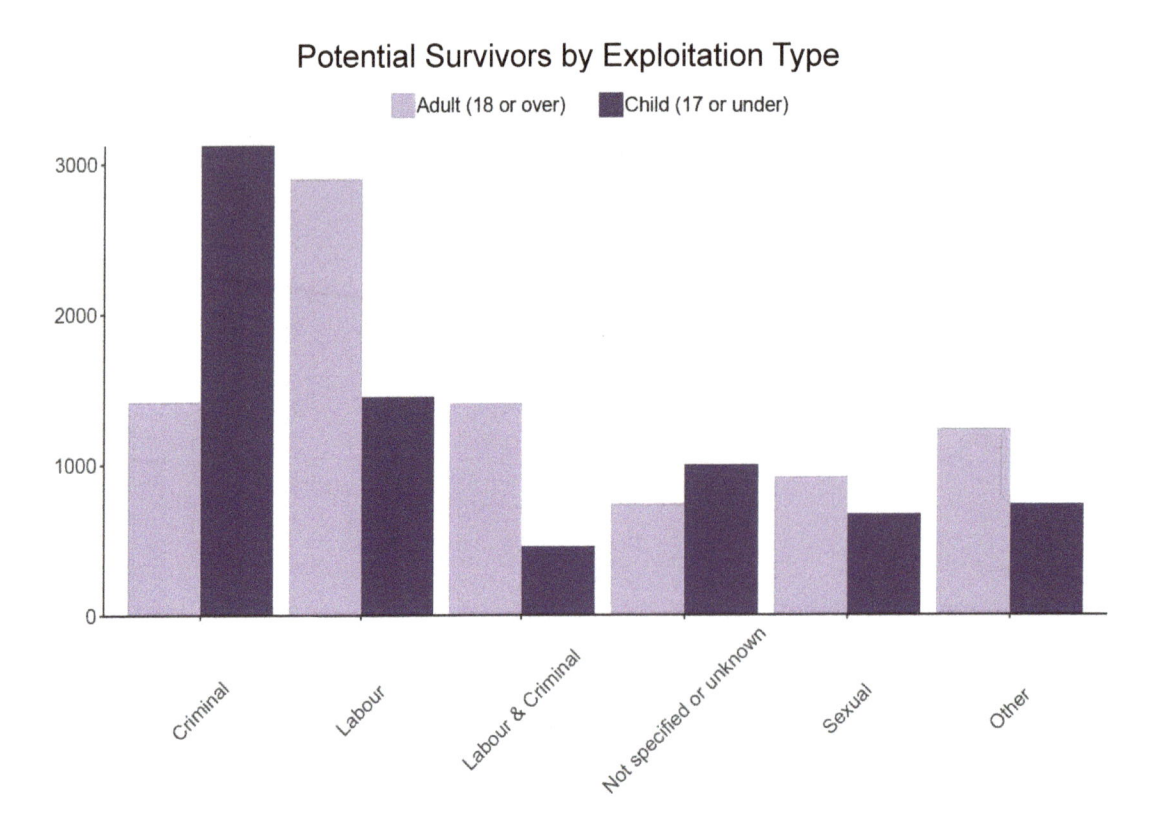

Potential Survivors by Exploitation Type

Potential Survivors by Nationality

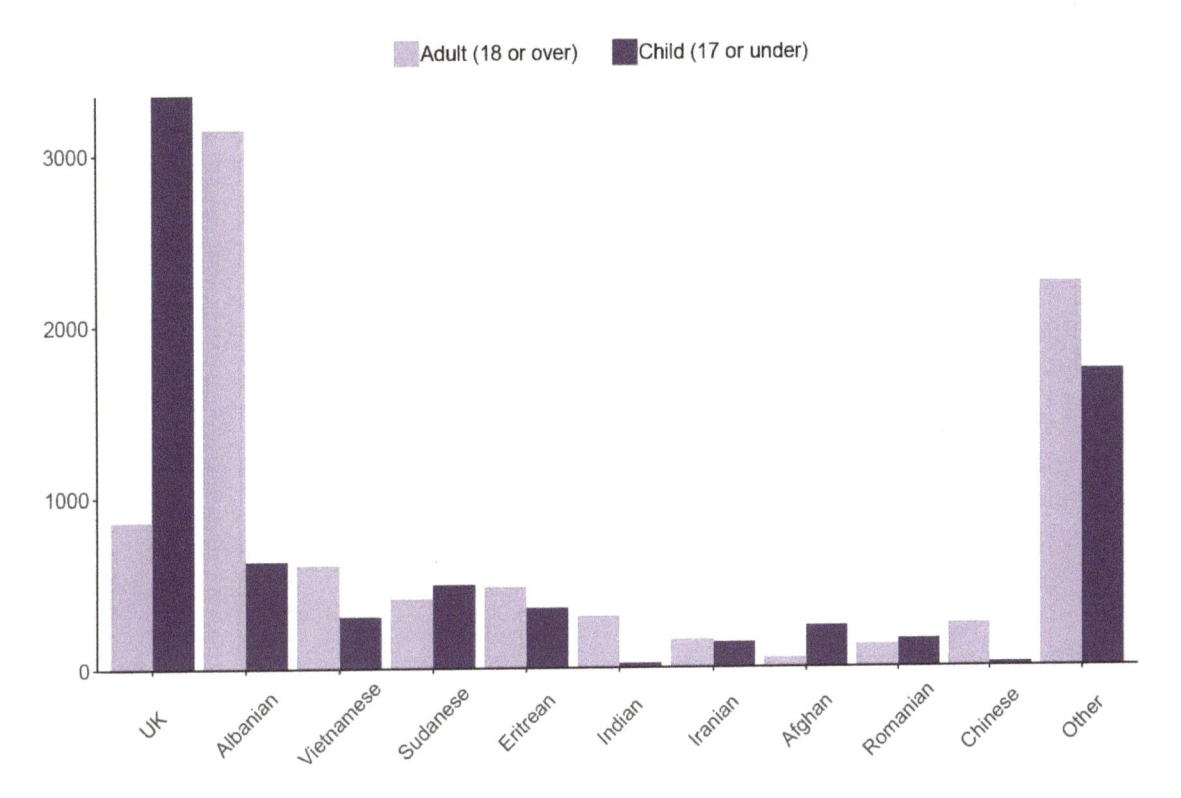

Tables have been obtained through: Modern Slavery: National Referral Mechanism and Duty to Notify statistics UK, end of year summary 2023 - GOV.UK (www.gov.uk). Please visit this website for more information.

The Liberty Project, BCHA

The National Referral Mechanism (NRM) is a vital framework designed to identify and support potential survivors of modern slavery and human trafficking. The Modern Slavery Victim Care Contract (MSVCC) is delivered by The Salvation Army, connecting survivors to specialised support providers like BCHA's Liberty Project.

At The Liberty Project, we empower survivors by providing comprehensive support in areas such as accommodation, legal services, criminal proceedings, mental health, physical health, training, and education for dependents. Our dedicated support workers tailor their approach to meet each survivor's unique needs, helping them break free from abuse and build the skills and confidence needed to live independently.

Amelia's story

Amelia was referred to The Liberty Project two years after being trafficked to the UK from her home country of Albania. Forced into an arranged marriage and assigned a fake ID, she was sent via Spain to Ireland. 'They told me this man would have to be my husband,' she said.

Aged just 25, Amelia's ordeal in Ireland lasted from September 2019 to April 2022, when she managed to escape while being transported by car. 'I ran so fast,' Amelia said. 'I ran and ran. I just wanted to get far away.'

Her bid for freedom couldn't have come at a worse time. The Covid-19 pandemic had just broken out and the UK had been placed in lockdown. Despite all odds, she managed to make it to the UK. Unable to speak English, she was fortunate to find someone who spoke Albanian and after asking for help, they took her in. 'I called immigration services and asked for their help, too,' Amelia explained. Following this, Amelia was referred to The Liberty Project for support.

Her caseworker said: 'When Amelia came to the service, she could not speak English, so all communication took place via translators. She was having nightmares because of the crimes she suffered and received therapy. Slowly, she started to develop and build up new skills while studying English and Maths, enrolling to take GCSEs. She has now studied accounting up to Level 2. The change from when Amelia arrived at service to when she left has been massive, and her life has experienced a remarkable turnaround. She has a partner, a 6-month-old baby, and Amelia is now fluent in English and is looking forward to developing her career. Her tale is proof that, despite a journey of abuse and despair, survivors provided with the right support can rebuild their lives.'

A Flavour of Liberty

The idea for this book originated from the heart of one of our female and children's safehouses, where survivors found joy and comfort in cooking for each other. Sharing recipes from their home countries became a cherished ritual, reminding them of home and helping them connect. New arrivals were always greeted with a home-cooked meal, easing their transition and welcoming them into the community. Inspired by this, the women decided to take their love of cooking beyond the safehouse to advocate for anti-slavery and highlight that modern slavery can happen anywhere. Thus, 'A Flavour of Liberty' was born.

Specialist Support Workers at Liberty embraced the cookbook project, integrating it into their keywork sessions with survivors. They met with survivors to discuss and select recipes from their home countries that would appeal to families, fostering valuable life skills in the process.

Through creating this book, survivors practiced their English by translating recipes, honed their math skills through measurements and conversions, and developed budgeting skills by ensuring the recipes were cost-effective. They also unleashed their creativity in designing the book's style and content and even sharpened their cooking skills by testing each recipe.

This book is more than a collection of dishes; it is a testament to resilience, connection, and the shared love of food that brings us all together. The survivors behind 'A Flavour of Liberty' hope you find as much joy in these recipes as they do!

All the recipes are handwritten by survivors, allowing this book to be authentic and in their own words.

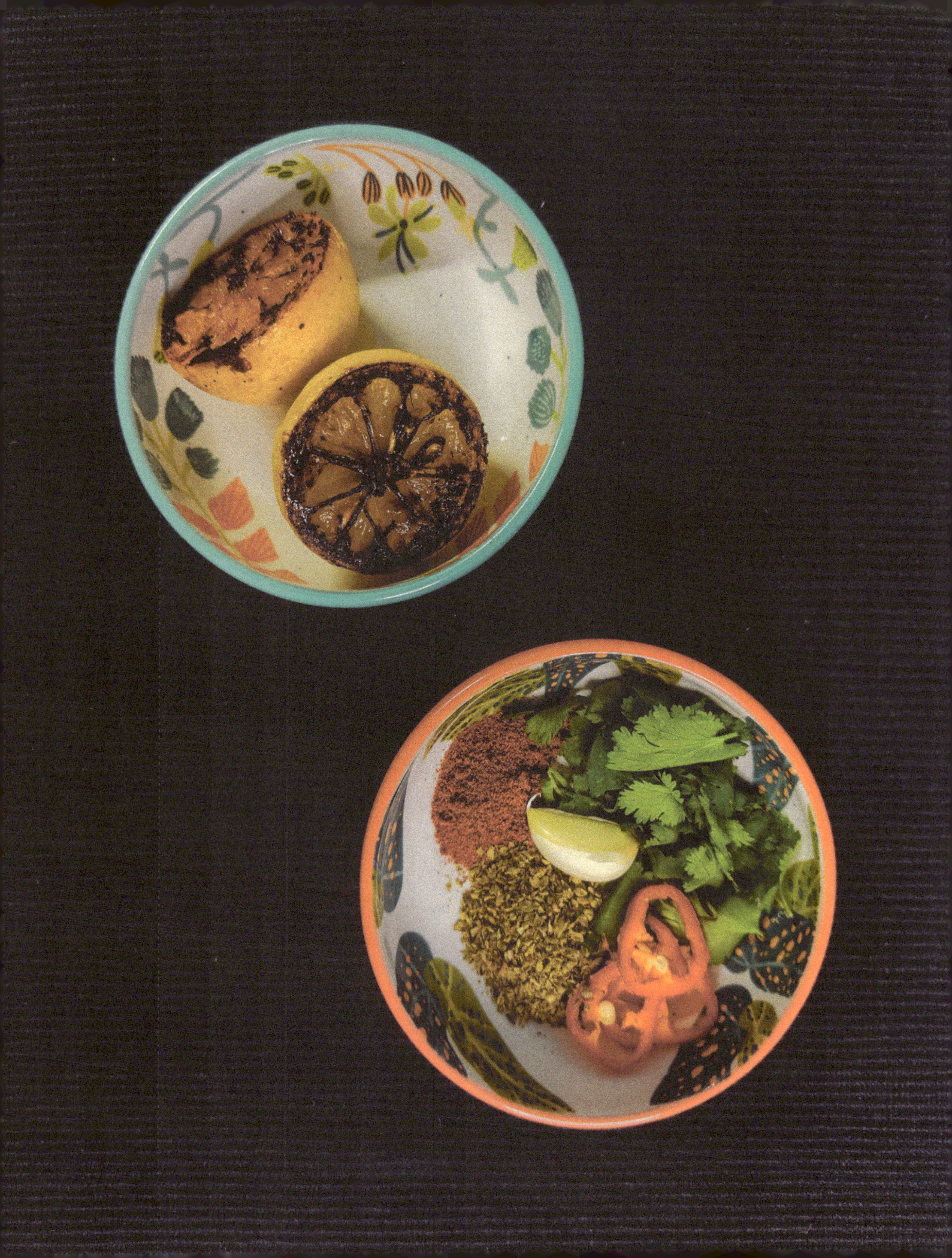

Mains

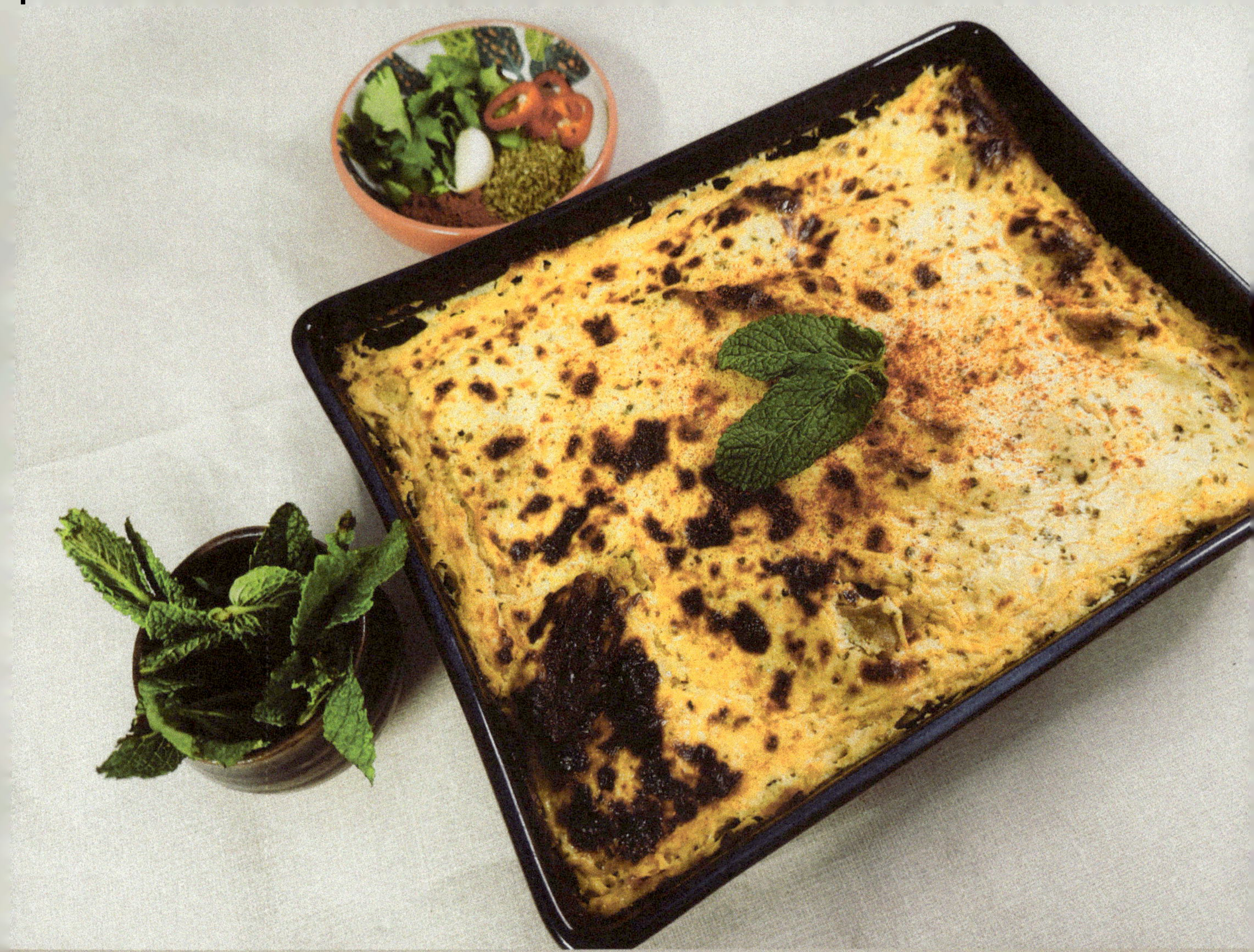

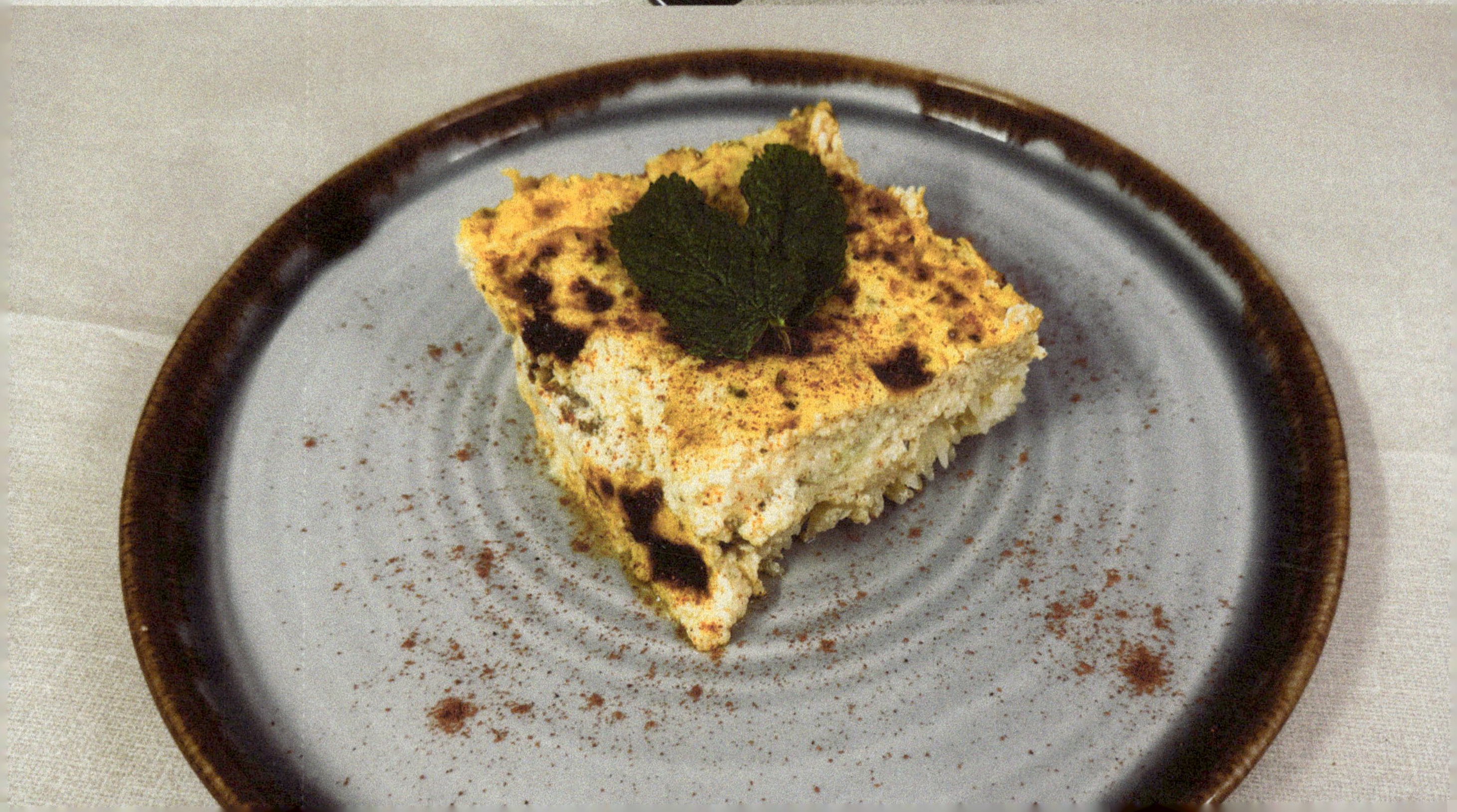

Albanian Tave Kosi – Lamb Yoghurt Dinner

Servings: 6
Prep Time: 15 minutes
Cook Time: 1 hour

Ingredients:

500g lamb chops/diced lamb. *Any meat can be used for this if lamb is too expensive, but lamb is the best choice for this dish.*
3 eggs
1kg plain yoghurt
2 tbsps. plain flour
100g rice
4 garlic cloves, grated
1 tsp oregano
1 tsp paprika
salt for seasoning
water – enough to cover the meat

Method:

1. Preheat the oven to 200°C.
2. Put the meat in a saucepan and add enough boiling water to cover it. Boil for 20 minutes.
3. While the meat is cooking, beat 3 eggs with a pinch of salt in a bowl.
4. Gradually add the flour to the beaten eggs and mix well.
5. Once all the flour is mixed in, add the yoghurt, paprika, garlic, and oregano. Mix well and set aside.
6. Once the meat has finished boiling, separate from the water. Keep the water as your stock and let it cool completely. It's extremely important the stock is well cooled before adding to yoghurt.
7. Spread the rice evenly at the bottom of an oven proof dish.
8. Carefully spread the meat on top of the rice.
9. Once the stock has cooled to lukewarm, mix it into the yoghurt mixture. The cooler the stock the better, as the hot liquid will ruin the yoghurt mixture if it curdles.
10. Pour the yoghurt mixture over the meat and rice, covering all the meat.
11. Sprinkle extra paprika on top of the meat and rice.
12. Bake in the preheated oven for 35–40 minutes, until the top is golden brown. Keep an eye on the colour as ovens may vary.

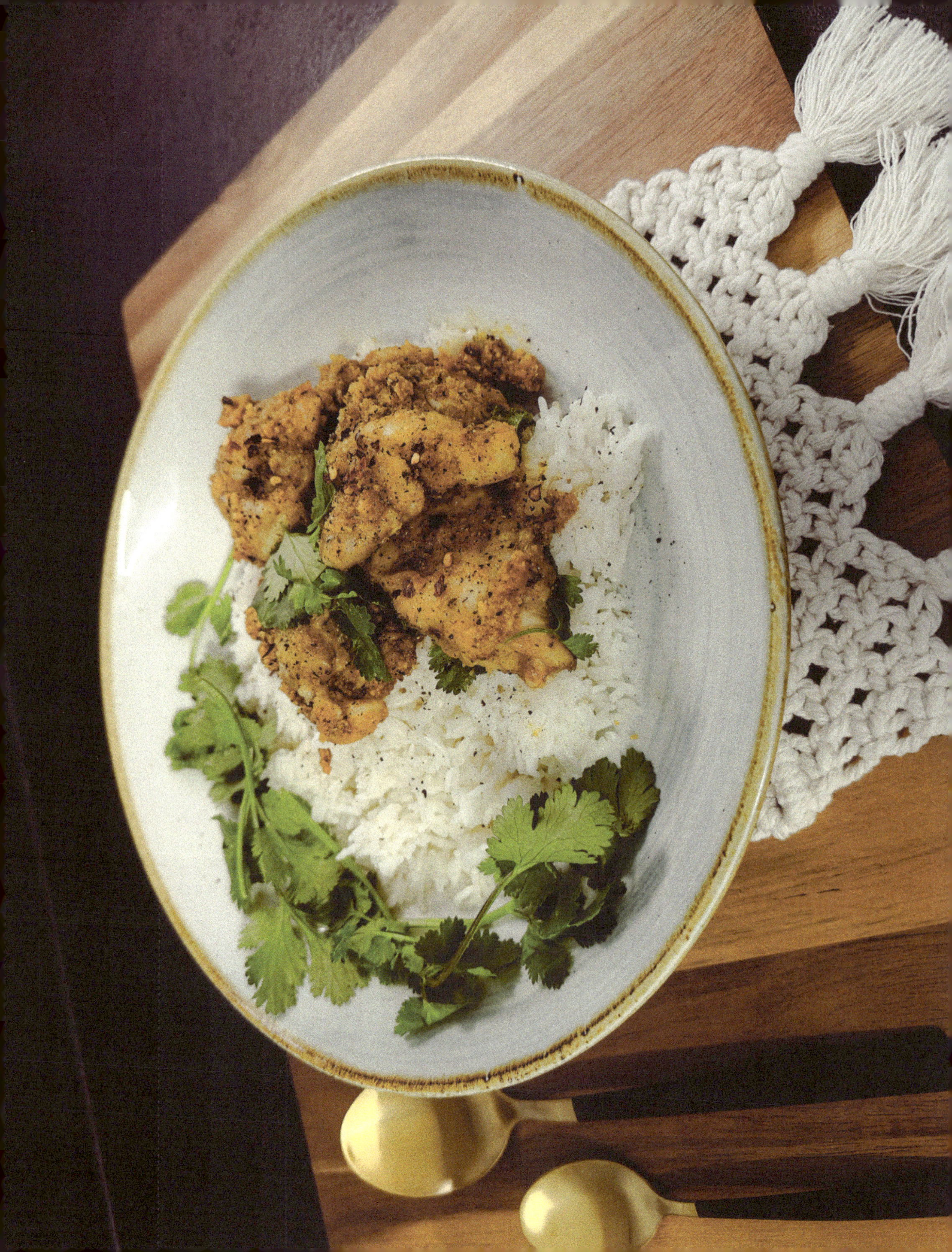

Albanian Tave Pulu – The Chicken dish

Servings: 4
Prep Time: 20 minutes
Cooking Time: 1 hour

Ingredients:

8x chicken thighs
100g butter
5 tbsps. plain flour
5 tbsps. corn flour
5 garlic cloves
oregano
½ tsp paprika
1x diced onion
salt and pepper – season to your own personal taste
water – enough to cover the meat

Method:

1. Pre-heat oven to 200°C.
2. Put the drumsticks in a saucepan with a lid. Add enough boiling water to cover the drumsticks, and 1/2 a teaspoon of salt. Set the heat to medium, cover, and boil for 20 minutes.
3. Whilst the chicken is boiling, you can begin the sauce. Get a frying pan, melt the butter with the onions. Cook until the onions start to turn golden brown.
4. Once turning brown, add the plain flour and corn flour. Stir continuously until the mixture is a medium brown colour, then switch off the heat and cover.
5. Once chicken is cooked, separate the chicken from the stock water. Place the chicken drumsticks in an oven proof dish and keep the water for later.
6. Gradually add the stock water to the sauce in the frying pan, stirring until you have a nice thick sauce.
7. Add the sauce from the frying pan, into the oven proof dish, coating all the drumsticks.
8. Grate your garlic into the dish and add your oregano and paprika. Stir gently, so the seasoning can be mixed into the dish.
9. Cover the dish with tin foil or a lid and bake in the preheated oven for 20 minutes.
10. Once cooked, remove from the oven, and serve with salad or vegetables of your choice.

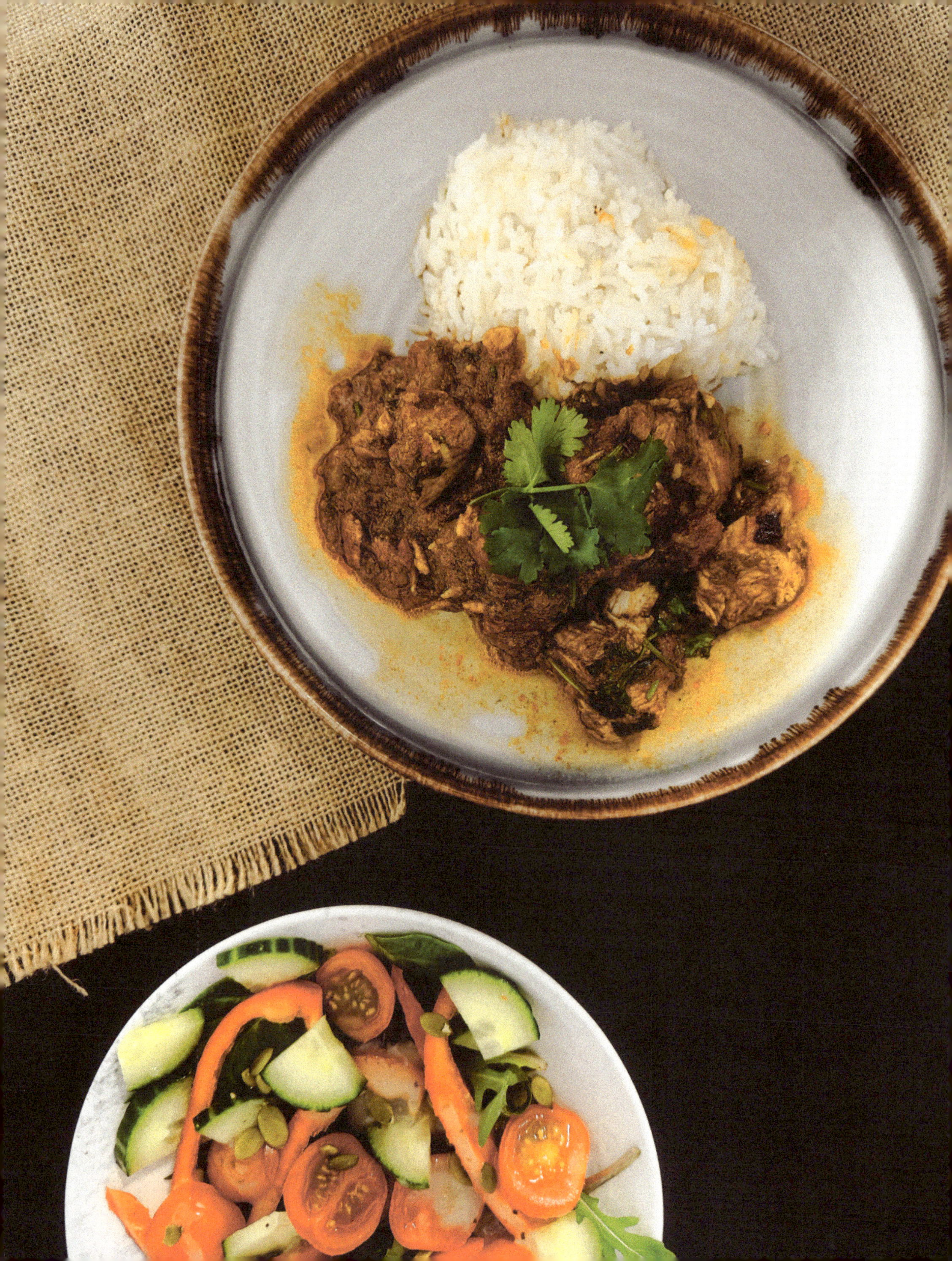

Bangladesh Chicken Curry

Servings: 6
Prep Time: 15 minutes
Cooking Time: 30–45 minutes (depending how soft you want the chicken)

Ingredients:

4x chicken breasts or diced chicken
1 tsp oil
1 tsp chilli flakes
1 tsp paprika
1 tsp coriander powder
1 tsp cumin
1 tsp curry powder
1 tsp cinnamon
1 tsp cardamom
2x garlic gloves grated
1 bay leaf
1 onion
1 litre of water
1x tin chopped tomatoes
salt to taste

We suggest you serve with peanut rice. Please see page 40 for this recipe.

Method:

1. Heat a large saucepan with oil.
2. Add the chicken and the spices – chilli flakes, paprika, coriander powder, cumin, and curry powder.
3. Fry until golden brown on the outside.
4. Add the onion and garlic, fry for a further couple of minutes.
5. Pour in the water.
6. Add the bay leaf, cinnamon, and cardamom.
7. Cook on a low heat for 30 minutes.
8. Serve with rice.

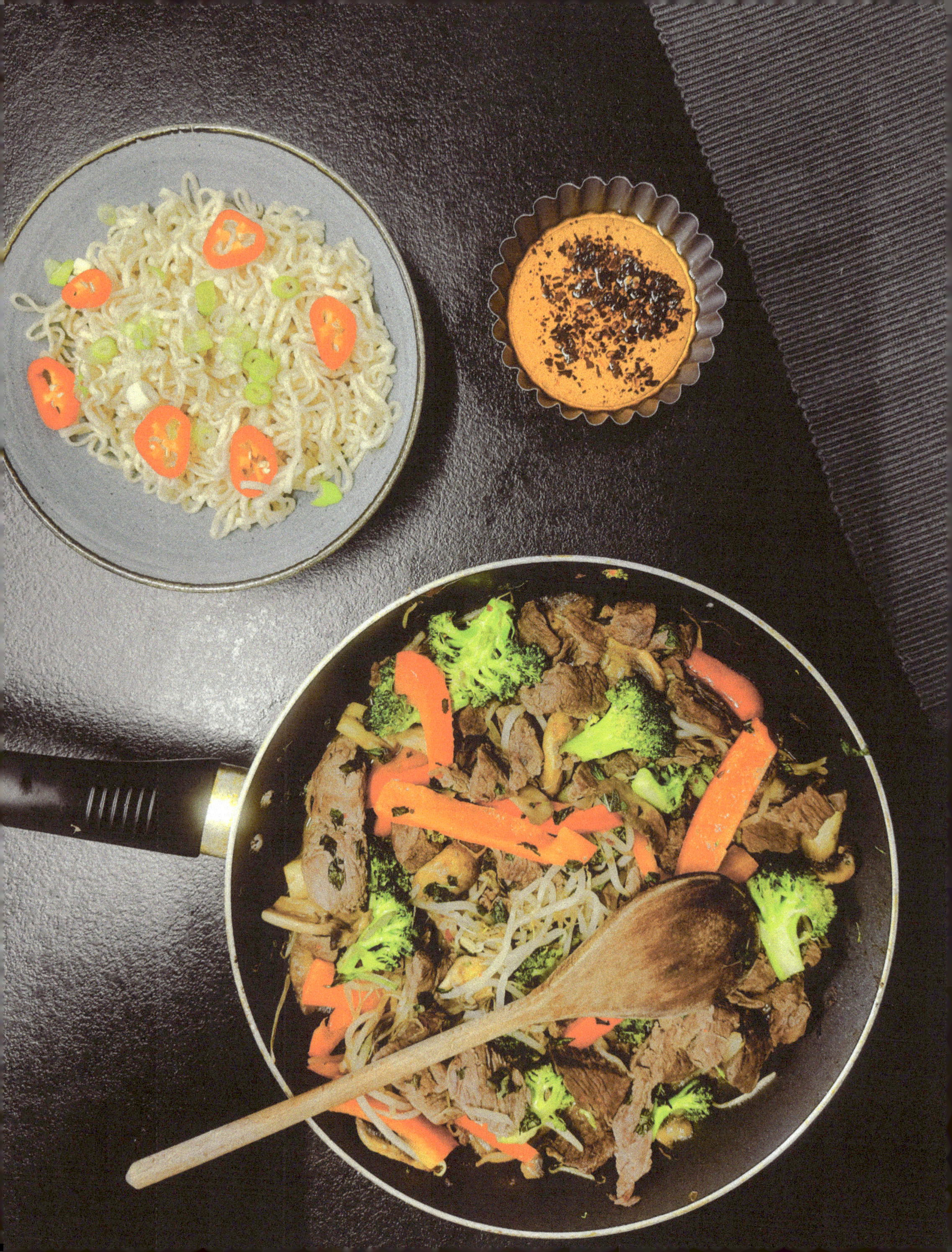

Chinese Stir fry Beef with Bamboo shoots

Servings: 4
Prep Time: 15 minutes
Cook Time: 20 minutes

Ingredients:

200g bamboo shoots
2 tbsp chilli paste
2 tbsp wok oil/veg oil
2 tbsps. fish sauce
1 tbsp chilli oil
3 garlic cloves grated
500g diced beef
300g mushrooms
½ a broccoli head
1x red pepper
bunch of basil leaves
1x chilli

Method:

1. Cut bamboo shoots into matchstick size.
2. Slice your mushrooms and broccoli into small pieces.
3. Add vegetable oil to a hot pan on a high heat.
4. Put the diced beef, mushrooms and broccoli into the pan and stir continuously for 5 minutes.
5. Add the chopped garlic, followed by the chilli paste and sauté for 1 minute.
6. Add the bamboo shoots and fish sauce and stir for approximately 1 minute.
7. This will cook medium/rare beef, cook for longer if you prefer your beef well done.
8. Roughly chop the basil leaves and toss them into the pan.
9. In a separate plan, fry the chilli.
10. Serve with steamed rice and garnish with basil leaves and fried chilli.

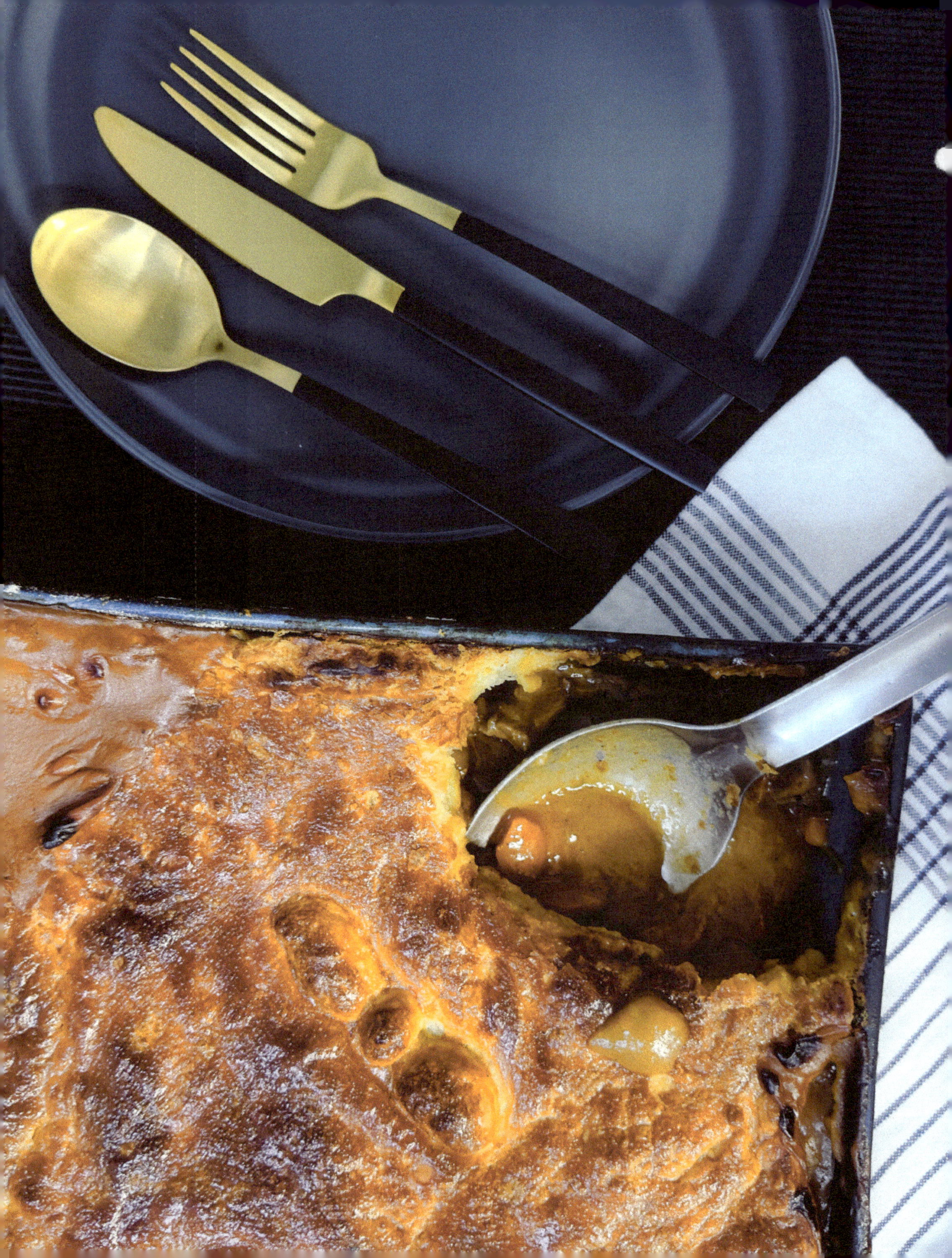

English Steak and Gravy Pie

Servings: 6
Prep Time: 15 minutes
Cooking Time: 3 hours

Ingredients:

1 tbsp sunflower oil
700g stewing beef
2 large onions – copped into large chunks
4 carrots – peeled and chopped
50g plain flour
2 tbsps. tomato puree
salt and pepper
600ml beef stock
2 tbsp Worcestershire sauce
320g puff pastry sheet
1 egg, beaten

Method:

1. Heat your oil in a large saucepan. Once hot, add the beef and cook for 5-10 minutes. You want your beef to be starting to brown.
2. Add the onion and the carrot, cook for a further 5 minutes, until the vegetables start to soften.
3. Add the flour and stir everything through. Cook for a further 5 minutes.
4. Add the tomato puree, Worcestershire sauce and stock. Season with salt and pepper. Put the lid back on and cook on a very low heat for about 2 hours. You want the beef to go nice and soft. Keep an eye on it and stir occasionally. If it looks like there is not enough liquid, add a little more water or stock.
5. Once cooked, put the mixture in a pie dish. Allow to cool for 30 minutes.
6. Smooth the puff pastry over the top of the filling. You can decorate with nice shapes if you wish.
7. Pre-heat your oven to 220°C.
8. Brush the top of your pie with the beaten egg.
9. Bake the pie for 30 minutes, until the middle is hot and the pastry is a crisp, golden brown.

We suggest you serve this with cheesy mash. Please see page 37 for this recipe.

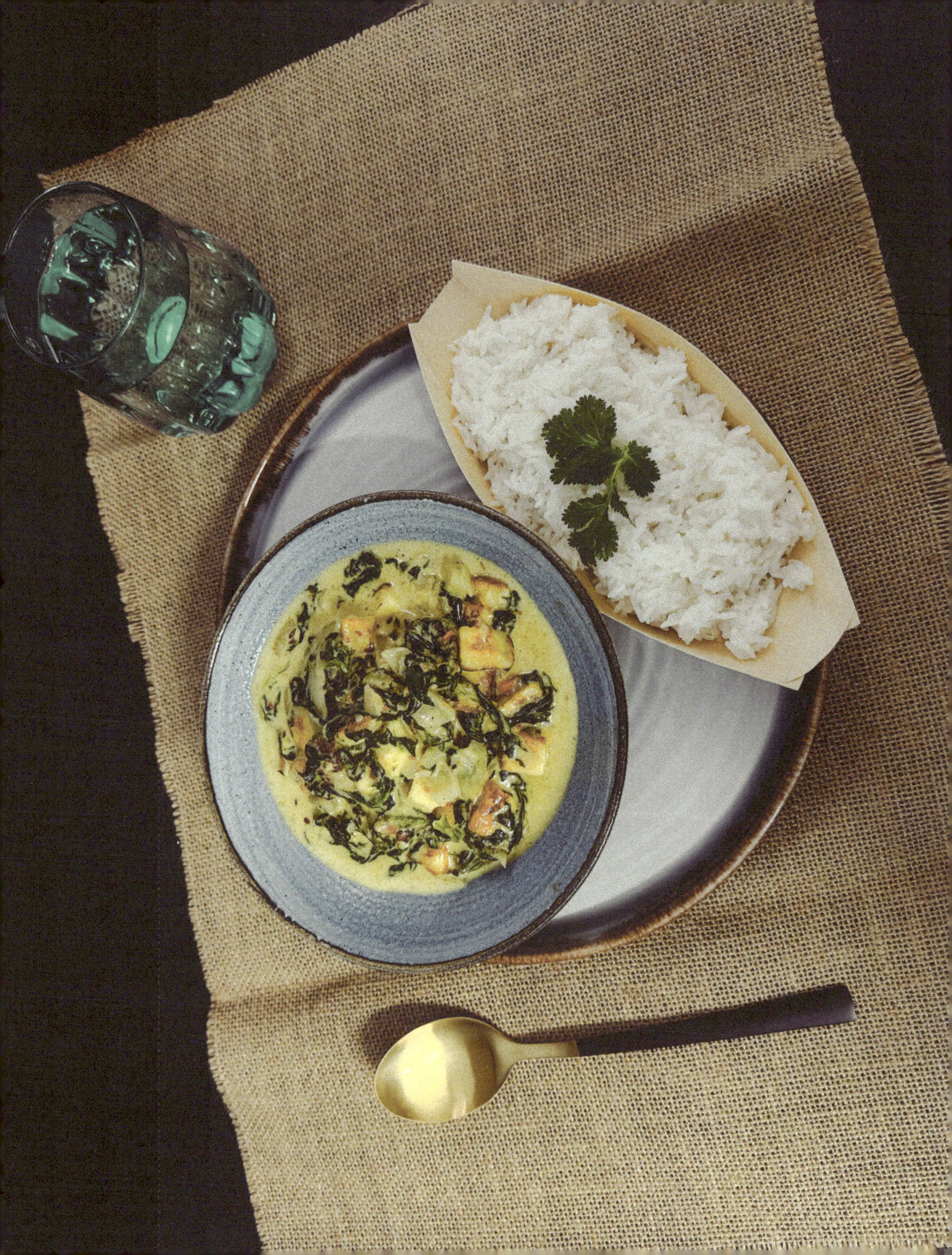

Indian Sag Paneer – Spinach and cheese curry

Servings: 4
Prep Time: 15 minutes
Cook Time: 45 minutes

Ingredients:

2 bunches spinach, roughly chopped
1 bunch fenugreek leaves, roughly chopped (can be substituted for watercress)
3 tbsp oil, divided
½ pound paneer cheese, cubed
1 tsp cumin seeds
1 onion, thinly sliced
3 cloves garlic, minced
1 tsp grated fresh ginger
1 tomato, diced
2 tsp garam masala
½ tsp ground turmeric
½ tsp cayenne pepper
½ cup heavy whipping cream
salt to taste

Method:

1. Bring a large saucepan of water to a boil.
2. Finely chop the spinach and the fenugreek. Add to the water and cook for 3 minutes.
3. Heat 1 tbsp of oil in a large pan over medium heat.
4. Add the paneer cubes and fry until golden brown, roughly 5 minutes. Transfer the paneer onto a plate and leave to one side.
5. Heat remaining 2 tbsps. of canola oil in the same pan over medium heat. Add cumin seeds and fry until lightly toasted.
6. Add the onion, stirring, until softened.
7. Add garlic and ginger and stir to coat.
8. Stir in the tomato, garam masala, turmeric and cayenne pepper. Cook until the tomato breaks down, stirring often, for about 10 minutes.
9. Stir in the spinach mixture, paneer cubes, and cream; add salt to taste. Reduce heat to low, cover, and simmer for 15 minutes, stirring occasionally.
10. Serve with steamed rice.

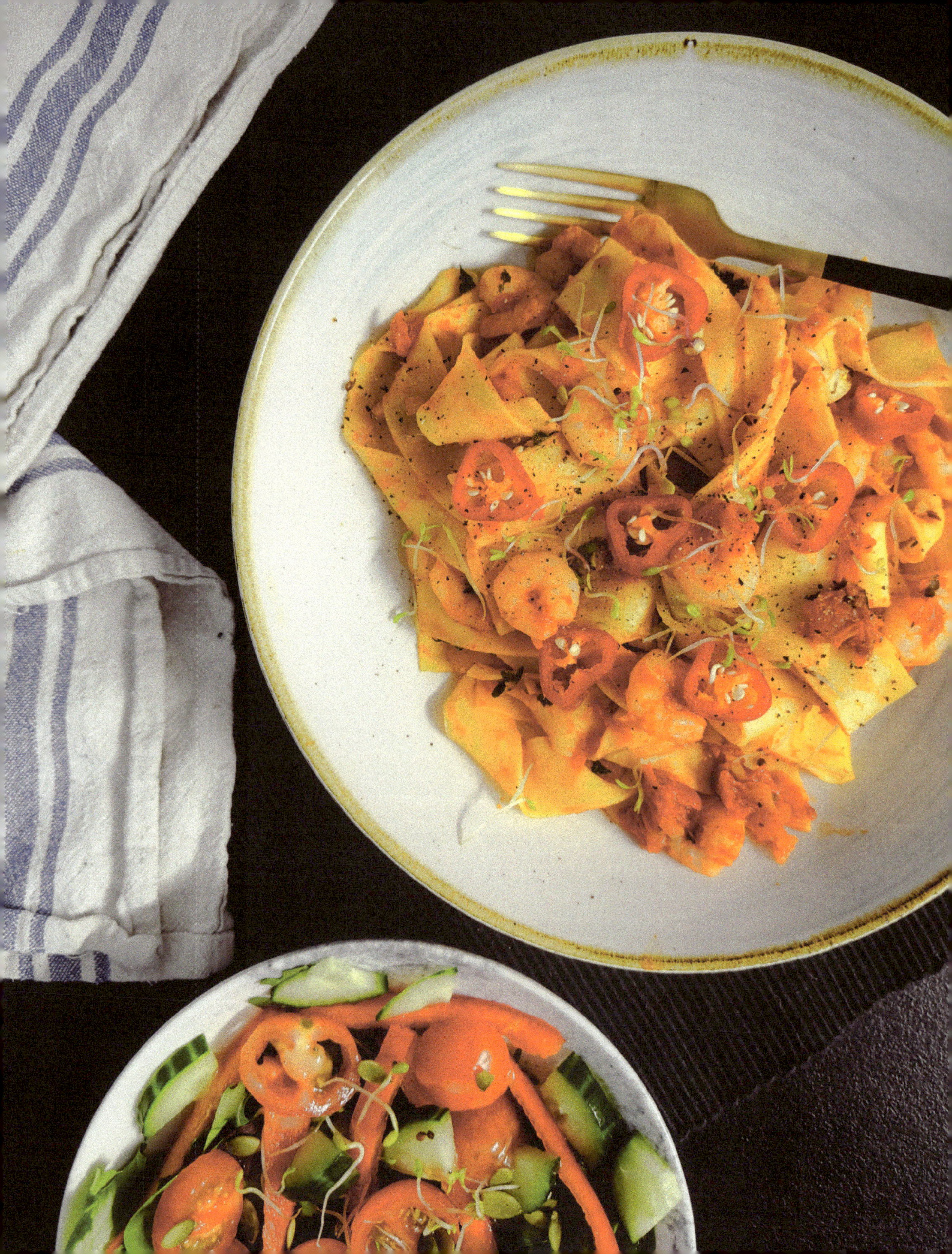

Italian Chilli Prawn Linguine

Servings: 4
Prep Time: 10 minutes
Cooking Time: 30 minutes

Ingredients:

2 tsps. olive oil
4 shallots, diced
2cms of ginger, grated
2 garlic cloves, crushed
2 tsps. of chilli flakes (add more if you like spicy food)
2x 400g tin of chopped tomatoes
300g linguine
bunch of fresh parsley
300g raw peeled prawns
fresh chilli to serve

Method:

1. Heat the oil in a large saucepan on a medium heat. Add the shallots and cook for 2 minutes.
2. Add the ginger, garlic, and chilli flakes. Cook for a further 2 minutes.
3. Add the chopped tomatoes, mix well, and let it all simmer for 20 minutes.
4. Meanwhile, put your linguine in boiling water, and cook in line with the instructions on the packet. Once cooked, drain the water.
5. Once your tomato mixture has simmered for 20 minutes, add the parsley and the prawns. Cook until the prawns turn pink.
6. Once the pasta and sauce have finished cooking, mix them together and serve.

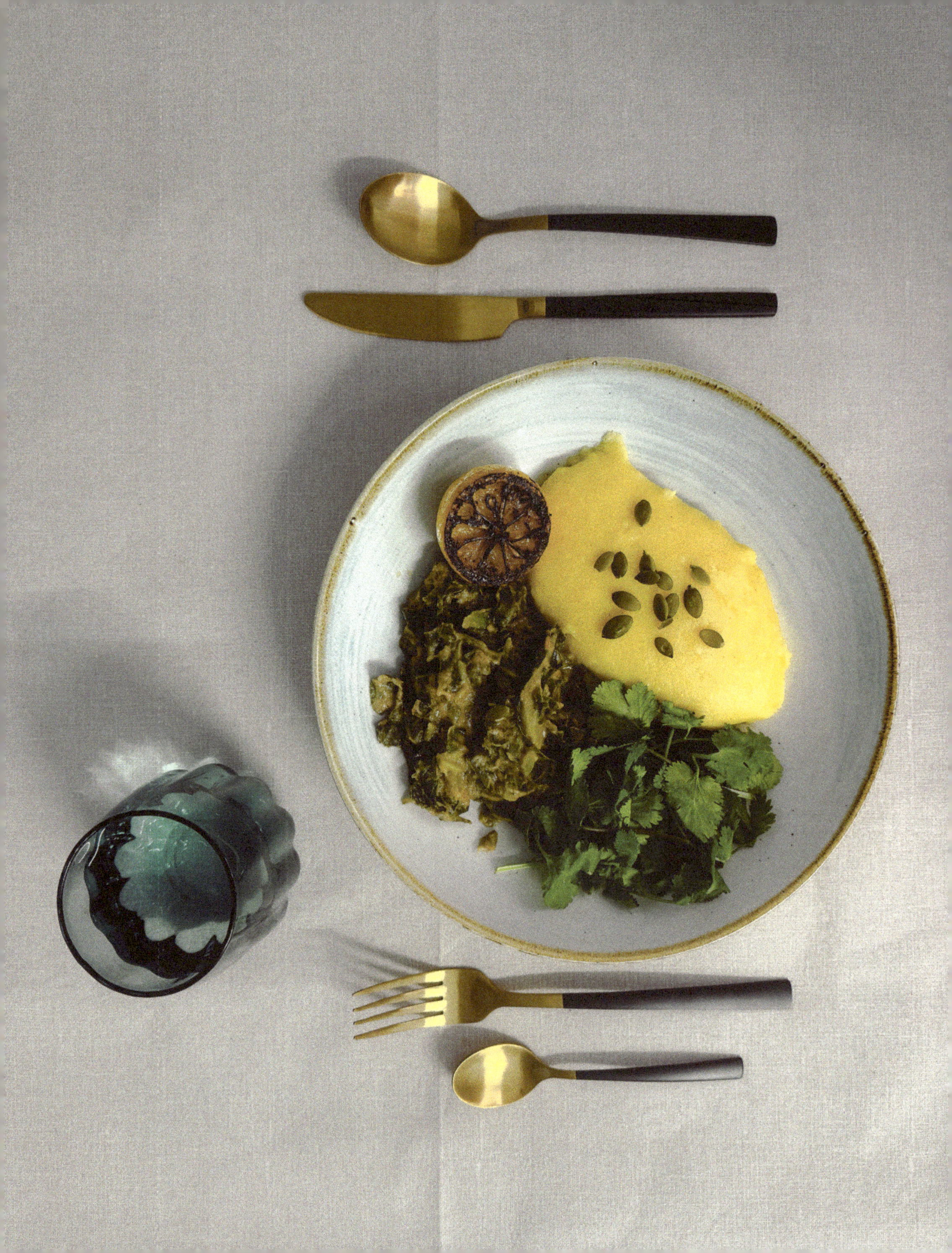

Malawian Ndiwo and Nsima – Relish Vegetables and Corn meal

Servings: 4
Prep Time: 15 minutes
Cooking Time: 45 minutes

Nisma – Corn Meal
Ingredients:

250g Maize flour
3 cups of water

Method

1. Warm up a large cooking pan for 4 to 5 minutes, to ensure it's hot before using it.
2. Add the water to the pan.
3. Gradually add the flour, whilst continually mixing until you get a thick porridge like mixture.
4. Keep mixing on the heat until it becomes thick and smooth. Once ready, you can dish up with the vegetable recipe below.

Ndiwo – Relish Vegetables
Ingredients:

500g chopped collard greens
1x chopped tomato
1 tsp peanut powder
240ml Water
1/2 tsp baking soda
1/4 tsp salt
1 cup of water

Method:

1. Pour 1 cup of water into a medium size cooking pot. Add the baking soda and stir until thoroughly dissolved. Place the pot on a hob at medium heat.
2. Add collard greens and tomato. Cook on medium to high heat for 5 to 8 minutes.
3. Add peanut powder, salt and more water if needed.
4. Stir thoroughly and lower the heat to low.
5. Cover and simmer for 15 to 20 minutes, stirring every 2 to 3 minutes to prevent the bottom from burning.
6. Service with the Nisma, corn meal recipe above.

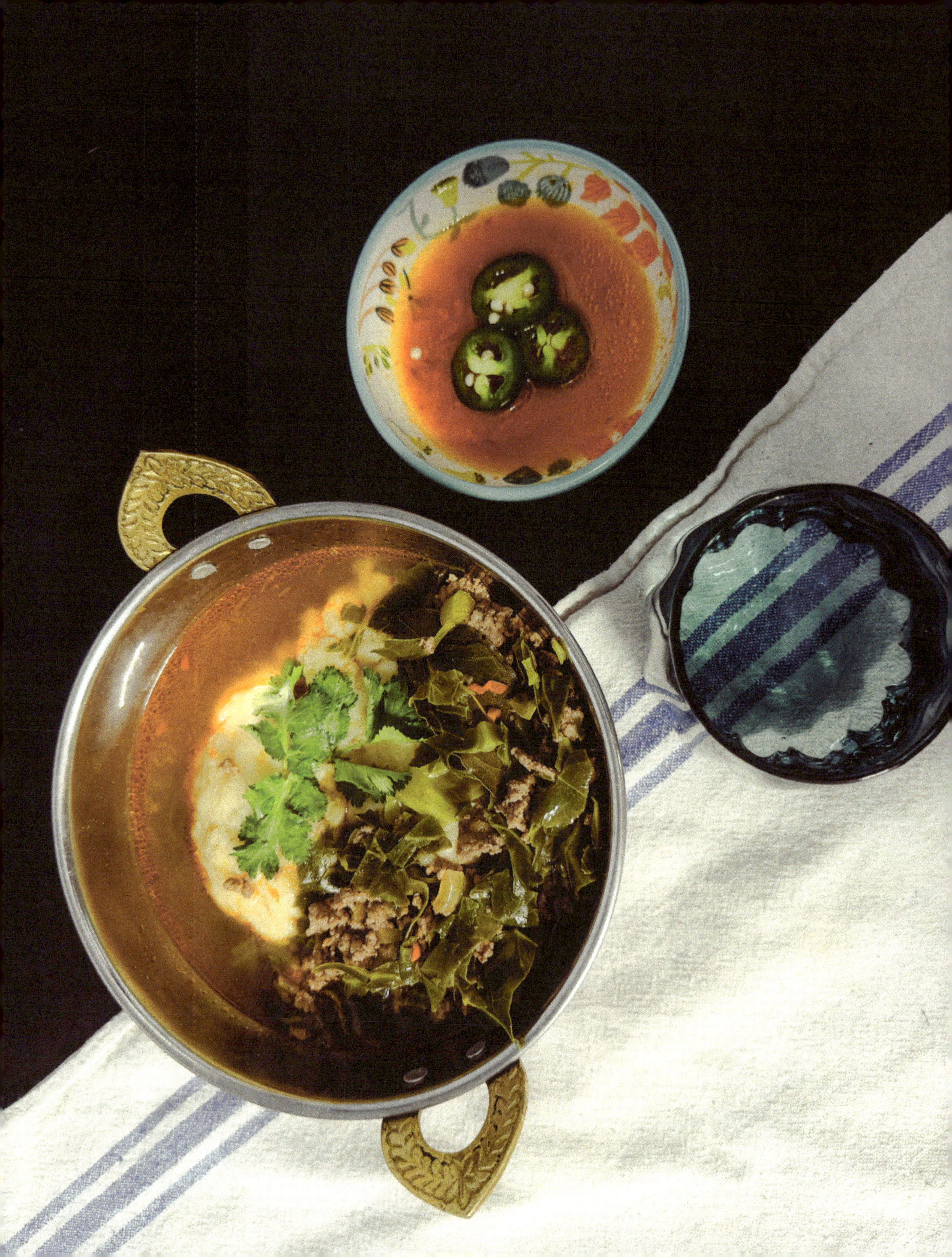

Nigerian Egusi Soup and Fufu – Melon Seed Stew and Dumplings

Servings: 4
Prep Time: 30 minutes
Cooking Time: 90 minutes

Ingredients:
<u>For the stock</u>
450g beef – You can use any meat or fish of your preference. Mackerel works well with this recipe.
1 red onion
2 tbsps. ground crayfish (can be substituted for fish oil)
2 tbsps. salt
½ tsp Nigerian red dry pepper (can be substituted for cayenne pepper)

<u>For the Egusi Soup</u>
1 red onion
½ a fresh habanero or scotch bonnet
300g ground egusi seeds (can be substituted for pumpkin seeds)
150g red palm oil
kosher salt and Nigerian red dry pepper
1 tsp ground crayfish
100g fresh pumpkin leaves or kale
100g fresh spinach

Stock Method:

1. In a medium pot mix the meat, onion, ground crayfish, salt and pepper, and 6 ½ cups of water. Bring to the boil.
2. Lower the heat after boiled and let the pot simmer for about 45 minutes until the meat is tender and the stock is slightly reduced.
3. Use a slotted spoon to remove the meat and transfer to a medium heatproof bowl and set aside.
4. Keep the stock.

Egusi Soup Method:

1. In a blender add onion, scotch bonnet and ¼ cup of water. Blend until it is a smooth texture.
2. Scrape into a medium bowl and stir in the ground egusi seeds.
3. Add water, 1 tablespoon at a time, until thick and creamy. This is your egusi paste. You can set aside.

4. In a large saucepan heat oil over a low heat for 1 minute.
5. Slowly add all the reserved stock and the crayfish.
6. Bring this to a gentle simmer. Add your egusi paste, 1 heaped teaspoon at a time and stir well.
7. Cover and cook. Gently stir this and scrape the bottom of the pan so it does not stick to it.
8. Cook for around 25 minutes until the paste is firm and crumbly.
9. Add the reserved beef and stir gently to break up the cooked paste into curds.
10. Season with salt and pepper to taste.
11. Continue to cook for around 10 minutes until the meat is heated through and tender.
12. Mound pumpkin leaves / kale on top of the soup without stirring. Then cover the pan and let it steam until the greens are wilted for about 2 minutes.
13. Now stir in the wilted greens and cook for about 8 minutes until they are soft.

Serve hot with either rice or FUFU (Recipe for FUFU below)

FUFU

Servings: 4
Prep Time: 10 minutes
Cooking Time: 15 minutes

Ingredients:
453g Yam powder
470ml Water

Method:

1. In a large pan boil 470ml of water. The pan needs to be large because the yam powder will expand.
2. Gradually mix in the yam powder. Slowly add this to the water in sections to avoid the yam powder going lumpy.
3. Stir the yam mixture until it goes thick and is smooth and stretchy.
4. Turn the heat off when the texture is thick and doughy.
5. Stir vigorously to get the best texture. Your arm will get tired but keep going as it will get the best results!
6. Wipe a bowl with water before adding the yam so it does not stick to the sides of the bowl.
7. Mould the yam into a bowl and serve with the Egusi Soup.

To eat, use clumps of the FUFU to pick up the soup with your hands.

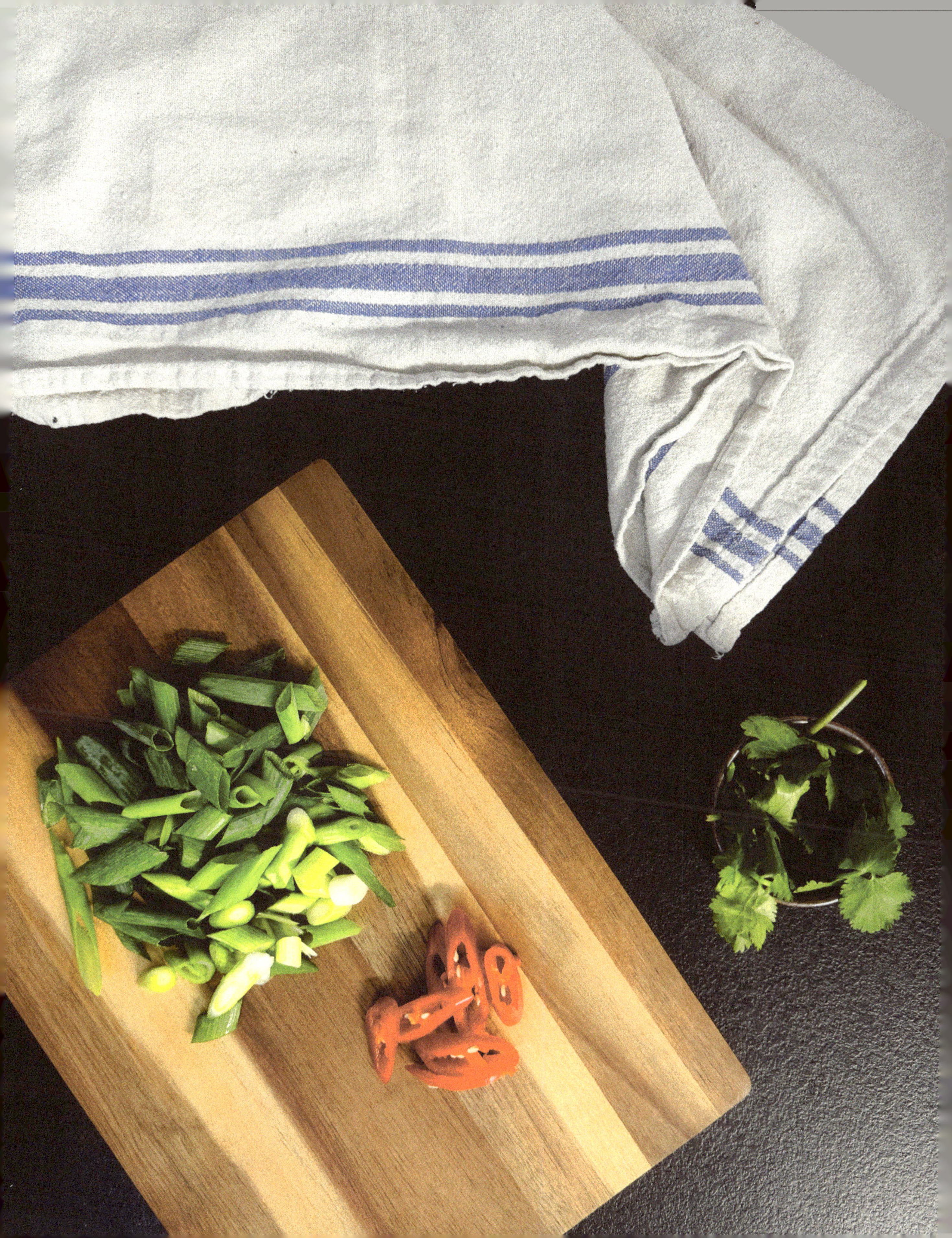

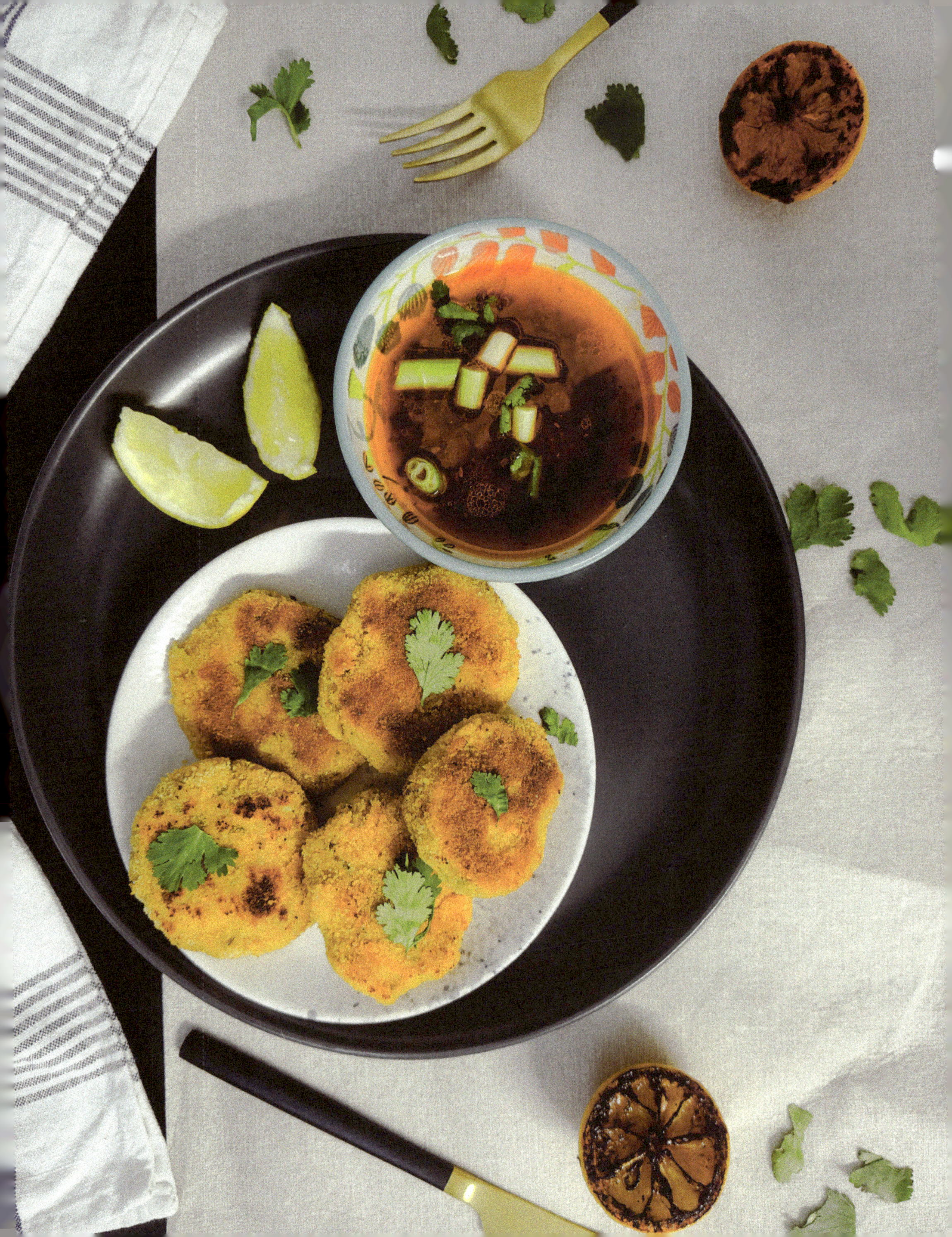

Pakistani Aloo Tikki – Curried potato street food

Servings: 4
Prep Time: 15 Minutes
Cook Time: 30 Minutes

Ingredients:
3 large potatoes
1 onion (red or white), roughly chopped
1–2 small chilli peppers, roughly chopped
2 tbsps. ground coriander
1 tsb coriander seeds
1 tbsp mint leaves
2 tsps. salt
½ tsp cumin seeds
½ tsp black pepper
½ tsp red chili flakes
½ tsp cumin power
¼ tsp chaat masala
¼tsp red chili powder
1 tsp lemon juice
¼ cup oil
3 eggs (2 whisked for the mixture, and 1 whisked for the breadcrumbs)
½cup breadcrumbs

Method:

1. Stab the potatoes with a fork. Place the potatoes on a microwave safe plate. Microwave on a high power for 5 minutes.
2. Turn the potatoes over and cook for a further 3 minutes. You want the fork to be able to easily slide through without resistance. Cook in 1-minute bursts until you reach this point.
3. Once cooked, leave them to cool until cool enough to handle. Then peel the potatoes and transfer the insides to a bowl.
4. Use a potato masher to mash them until smooth. Put to one side.
5. Place all the remaining ingredients, apart from the egg, into a food processor. Use the pulse function to chop so that everything is finely chopped, but not blended.
6. If you do not have a processor, you can finely chop by hand, and then mix together.
7. Now add this mixture to the mashed potatoes. Mix and combine everything together.
8. Taste and adjust seasoning if needed. You can add more salt, chilli etc.
9. Whisk 2 of your eggs and add them to the mixture. Mix well until combined.
10. Ideally, leave to rest for 20 minutes in the refrigerator. However, you can skip this if needed.

11. Using your hands, shape around ¼ of a cup's worth of mixture into a patty shape. Around half an inch thick, and 2 to 3 inches in diameter.
12. If the patties are not holding shape, or are too soft, you can add some breadcrumbs to thicken.
13. Put your patties to one side.
14. Whisk your third egg in a bowl.
15. In a separate bowl, add your breadcrumbs.
16. You can now dip your patty in the egg mixture, and then coat in the breadcrumbs.
17. Repeat these steps until all the patties are covered.
18. Heat a large saucepan over a medium heat and add some oil.
19. Place the patties in the pan and cook for 3 to 4 minutes on each side, using a spatula to turn them. Cook until golden brown.
20. Once cooked, transfer the patties onto a paper towel lined plate.
21. Repeat until all patties are cooked. You can cook around 4 to 5 at a time.

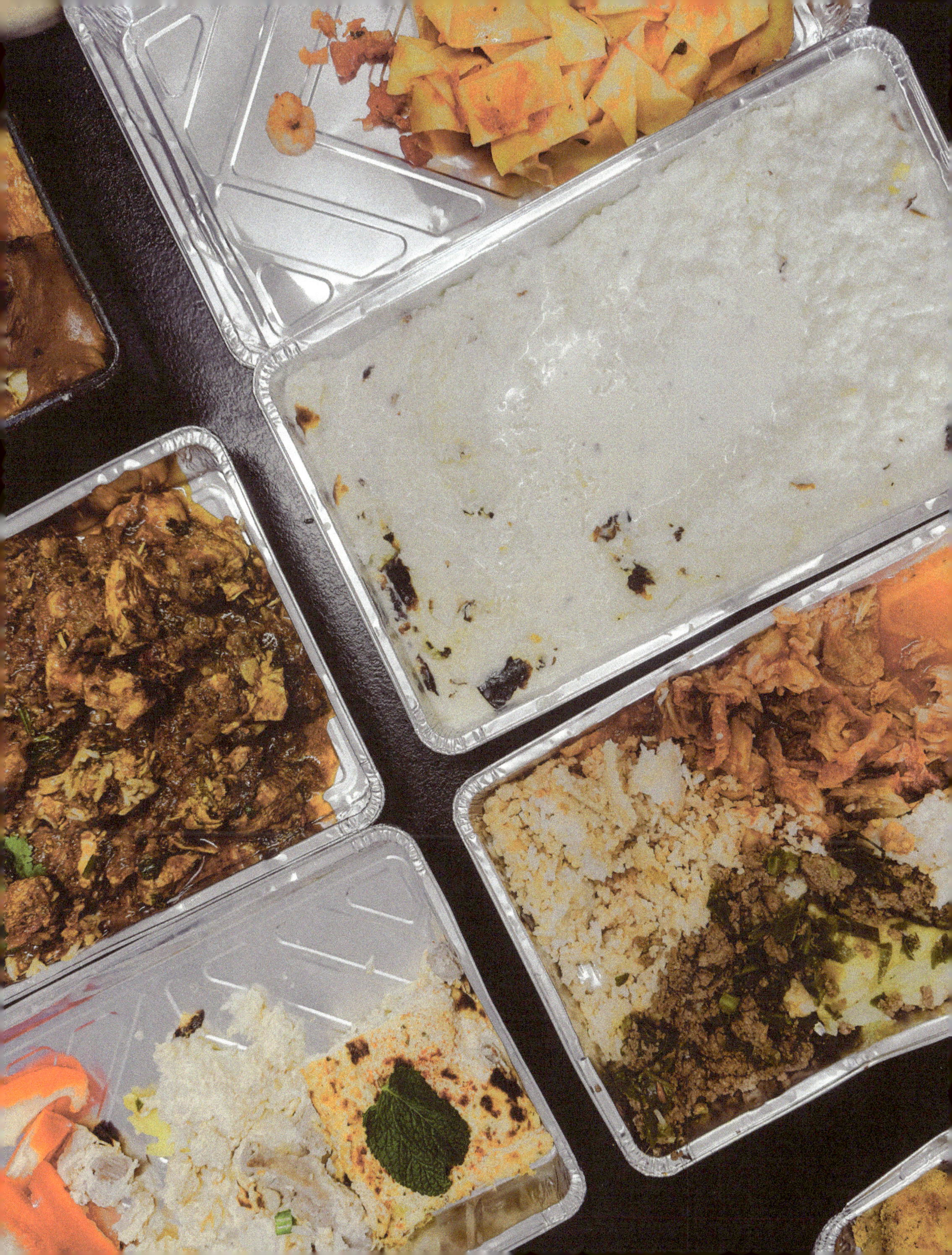

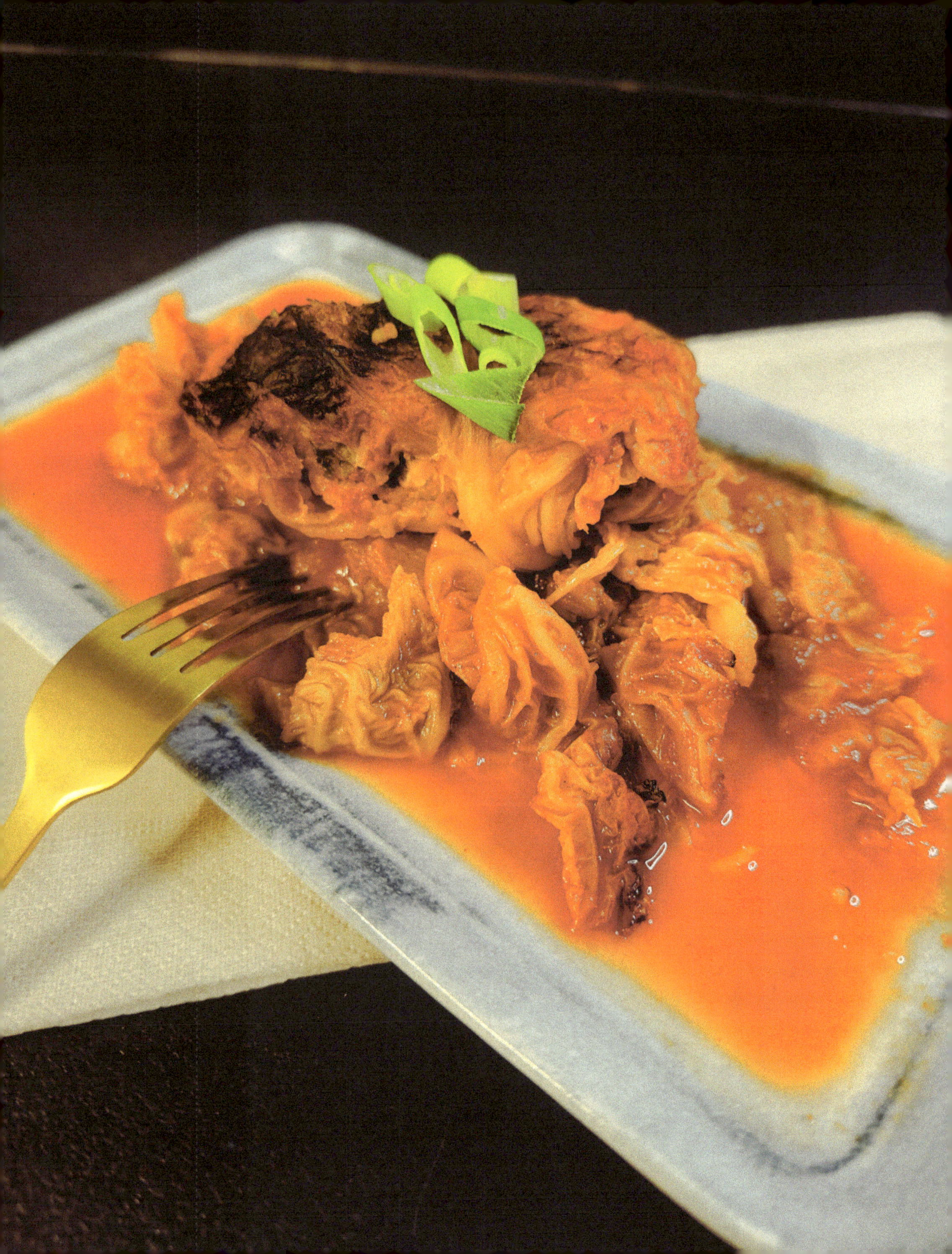

Romanian Cabbage Rolls – Sarmale

Servings: 6
Prep Time: 30 Minutes
Cooking Time: 2 Hours

Ingredients:
2 tbsps. vegetable oil
1 large onion
60g cup long grain rice
30g cup of parsley
30g cup of dill
salt and pepper to taste
1 cabbage
1 litre of tomato juice
water as needed
1 egg
450g minced meat – turkey, chicken, or pork. We suggest using chicken mince.
1 x chicken seasoning

Method:
1. Boil the full cabbage in salted water for 15 to 20 minutes.
2. Wait for cabbage to soften and then take it out and place on a plate.
3. Peel off the leaves gently and leave them to cool down.
4. Heat oil in a pan and fry the chopped onion. Cook until softened, then add the rice and cook for another minute.
5. In a large bowl add the meat, salt and pepper, parsley, dill, and then onion rice mixture.
6. Do not add too much salt as the cabbage is already salty. Mix this well using clean hands.
7. Preheat oven to 190°C.
8. Fill each cabbage leaf with a small amount of the meat mixture. Just enough to fill the centre in a sausage shape.
9. Then roll it tight and tuck in the ends, like a wrapping a fajita. Repeat this with all the cabbage leaves.
10. With the remaining cabbage leaves, cut them up, and layer them at the bottom of a baking dish.
11. Place your rolls on top of the chopped cabbage.
12. In a separate bowl, mix the tomato juice with boiling water (dependent on dish size). Enough water to cover your cabbage rolls.
13. Now pour this mixture into the baking tray.
14. Bake for 2 hours.

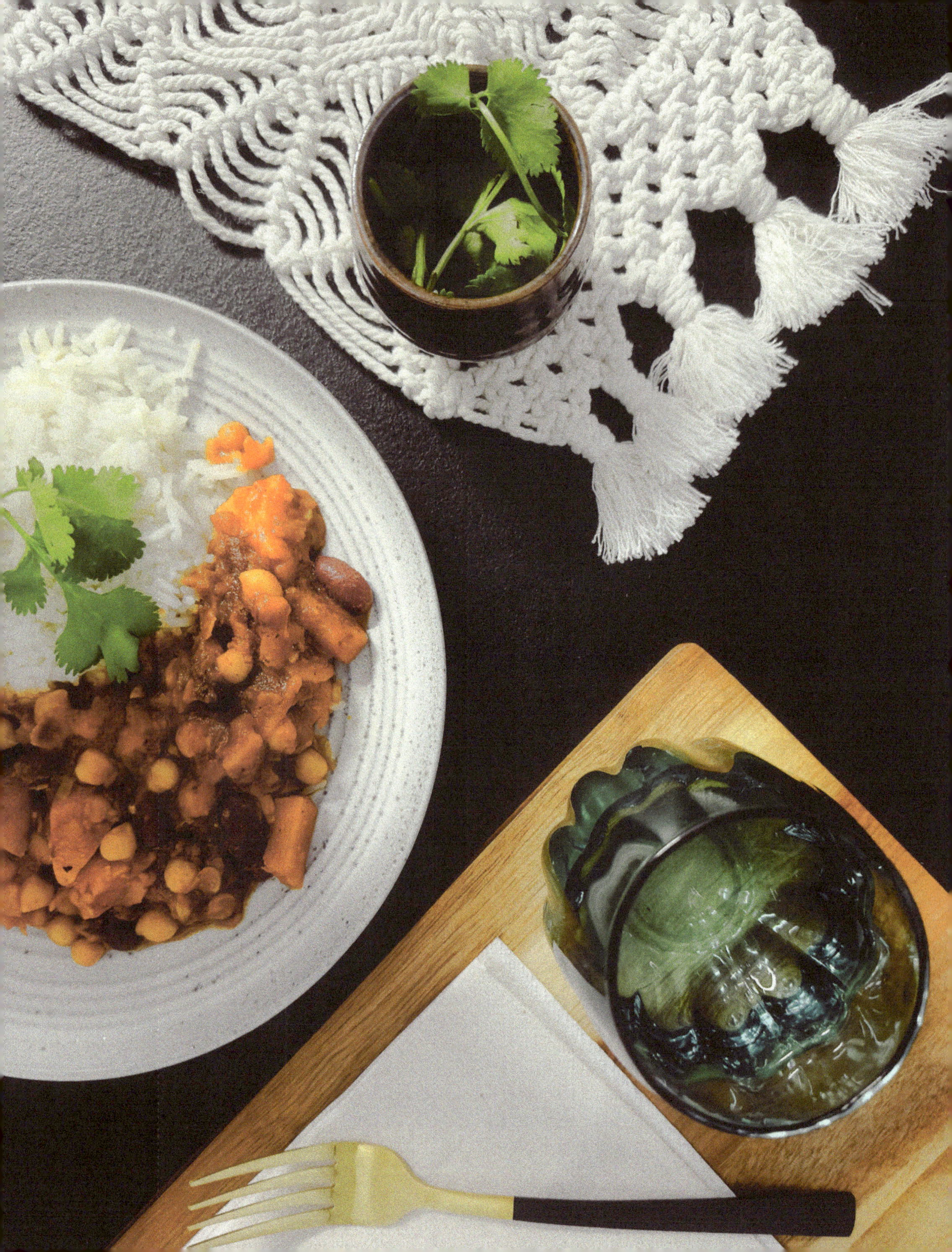

South African Sweet Potato Hotpot

Servings: 6
Prep Time: 15 minutes
Cook Time: 30 to 45mins

Ingredients:

2 sweet potatoes, cut in small cubes
1 onion, diced
½ bunch of spring onions, chopped
1 tsp ground cumin
1 tsp whole cumin
1 tsp ground coriander
1 tsp garam masala
1 tsp smoked paprika
500g passata
1 tin kidney beans
1 tsp chilli flakes
1 tin chickpeas
bunch of coriander
parsley to garnish

Method:

1. Put some oil in a saucepan on a medium heat and wait for the oil to heat up.
2. Add in the whole cumin, ground cumin, garam masala, ground coriander and the smoked Paprika.
3. Add in half a bunch of chopped spring onions and one onion.
4. Sprinkle the coriander and infuse for 1 minute.
5. Add in the sweet potato with a pinch of salt and mix together.
6. Once coated nicely add in the passata, chickpeas and kidney beans.
7. Top with water until it is covered.
8. Bring to the boil and let it cook for 30 to 45 minutes, until the sweet potato is nice and soft
9. Serve hot, garnish with parsley and serve with rice, flat bread or couscous.
10. Enjoy with good company!

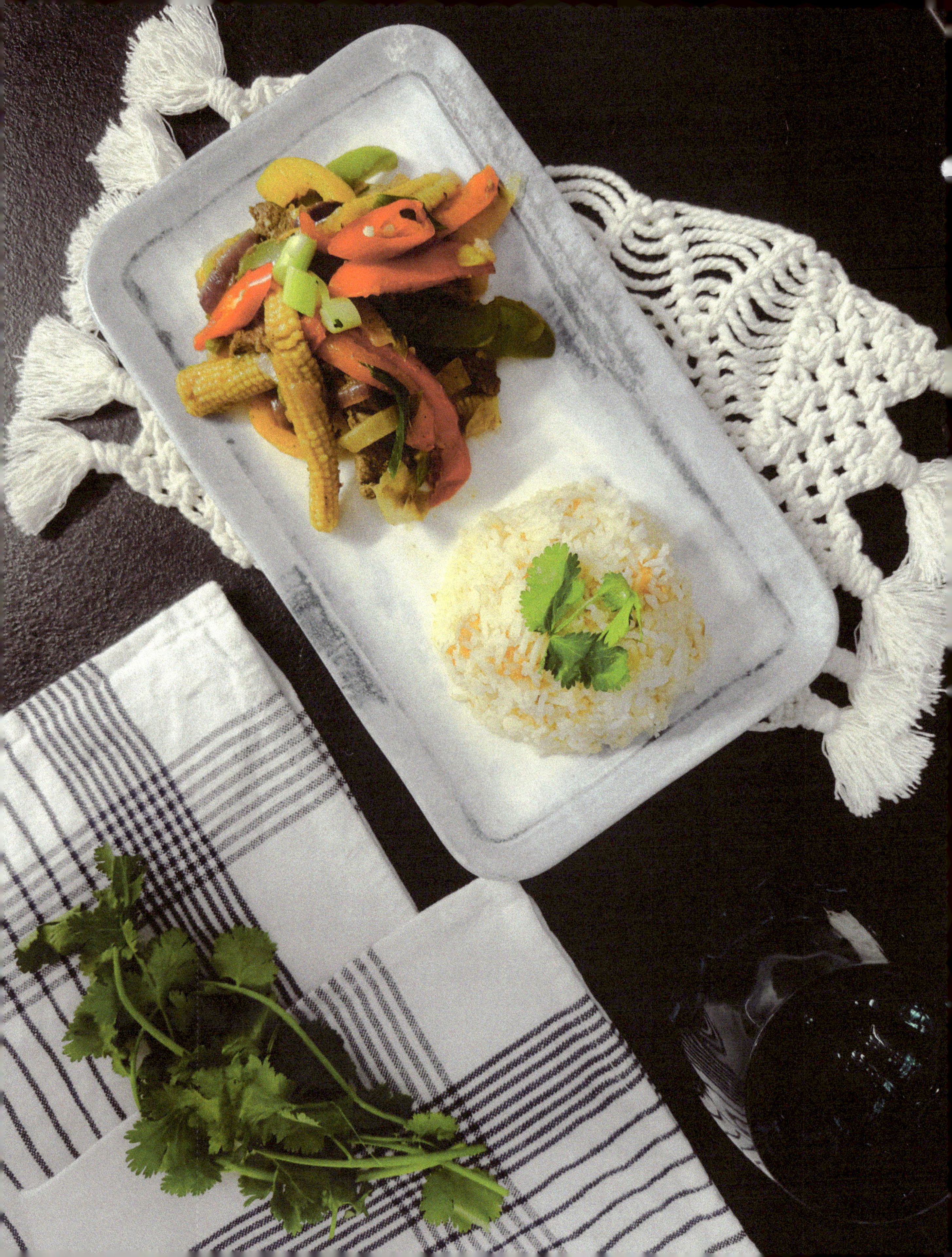

Zimbabwean Stir-Fried Beef

Servings: 6
Prep Time: 20 minutes
Cooking Time: 15 minutes

Ingredients:

700g diced beef
1x fresh ginger (roughly 3cm)
3x garlic cloves, grated
bunch of spring onions
1 tbsp all spice
½ chilli
salt and pepper to taste
2x onions
3x peppers – a green, yellow and red
150g mini corns

Method:

1. It's best to marinate your meet 24 hours before cooking. However, if you do not have time, you can do it just before. But for a strong flavour, marinate for several hours.
2. To marinate the meat, put all the spices in a large bowl and mix together. Then put your meat in the bowl and mix until all the meat is evenly coated.
3. Once you're ready to cook, heat a large frying pan on a medium heat with some oil.
4. Add your marinated meat to the pan, continuously stirring it for a couple of minutes. You can reduce the time for rarer meat or increase if you'd like it well done. A couple of minutes will produce medium meat as the result.
5. Then add the onions, peppers, and mini corn and stir fry everything together for around 8 minutes.
6. Once cooked to your liking, it's ready to serve.

We recommend serving with peanut rice. The recipe for this can be found on page 40.

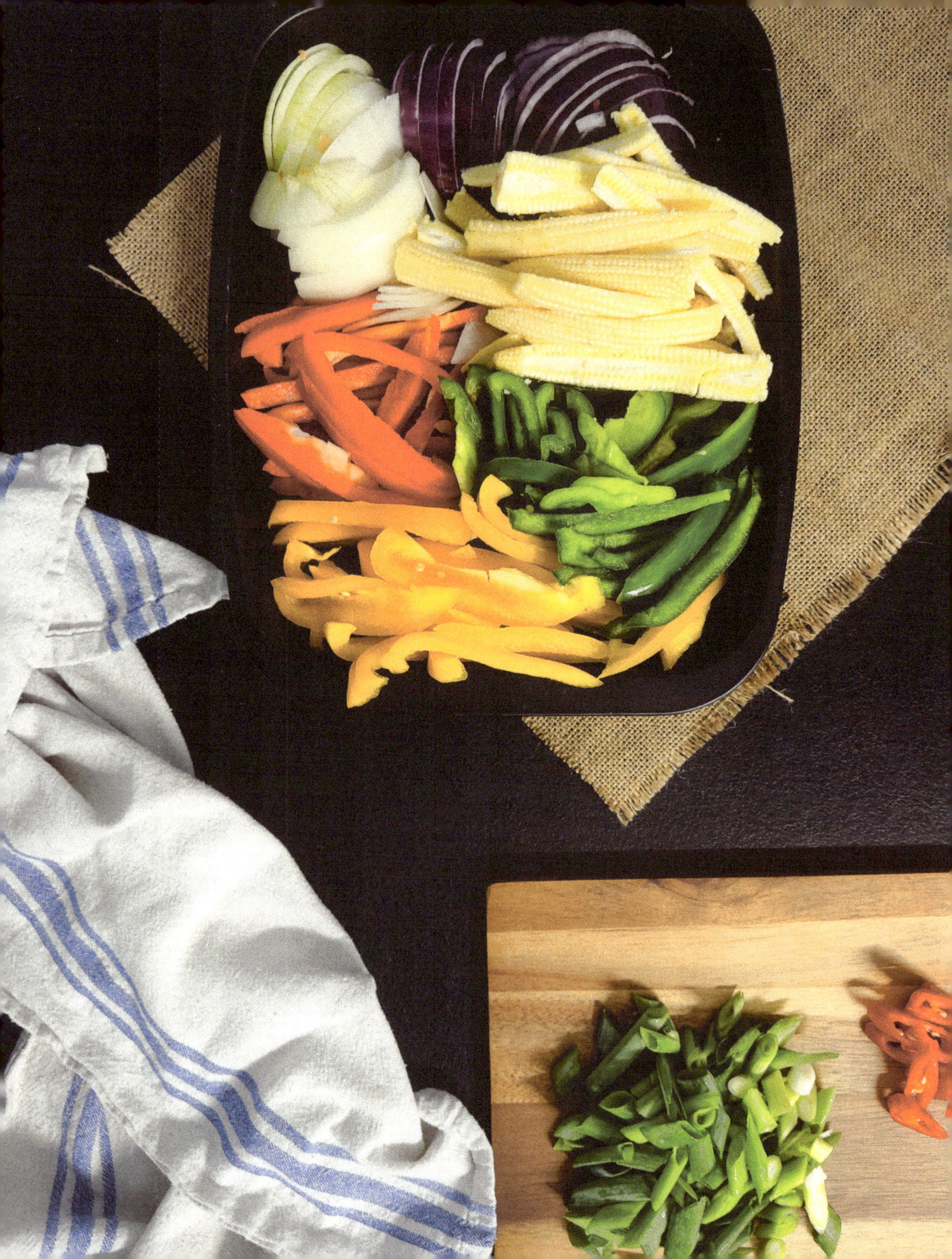

Sides

British Cheesy Mash

Servings: 6
Prep Time: 10 Minutes
Cooking Time: 20 Minutes

Ingredients:

1.5kg of peeled potatoes, cut into cubes
salt and pepper to taste
60g butter
50ml milk
80g cheddar cheese, grated
30g parmesan cheese, grated (you can substitute for more cheddar for a cheaper option)
100g soft cheese

Method:

1. Put the potatoes in a large saucepan and cover with water. Add a pinch of salt.
2. Bring the pan to a boil, once boiling, reduce to a medium heat.
3. Cook for 15 minutes, until the potatoes are tender. Drain the potatoes and return them to the pan.
4. Put the heat back on to a medium heat, cover the pan with a lid, and let the potatoes steam for 2 minutes.
5. Turn the heat off and mash the potatoes with a potato masher until smooth.
6. Add all the butter and half the milk. Stir until combined.
7. Slowly add the remaining milk. You may not need it all, you want the potatoes to be creamy but not watery.
8. Add the cheese, more salt and pepper, and mix together.
9. Serve immediately.

Mexican Paprika Potato Wedges

Servings: 4
Prep Time: 10 Minutes
Cooking Time: 30 to 35 Minutes

Ingredients:

4 large potatoes
1 tsp smoked paprika
3 tbsps. oil
salt

Method:

1. Cut each unpeeled potato in half lengthways, then slice each half into four long wedges.
2. Put the potatoes in a large saucepan with boiling water, boil on a low heat for 5 minutes.
3. Meanwhile, pre-heat your oven to 200°C.
4. In a separate bowl, mix the oil, paprika and salt.
5. Once your potatoes have boiled, drain them, and leave them to steam in the colander for a few minutes.
6. Put the potatoes in the bowl with the seasoning and coat all the wedges.
7. Scatter the wedges in a single layer on a baking tray and bake in the oven for 25 to 30 minutes

Thai Roasted Vegetables

Servings: 6
Prep Time: 15 Minutes
Cooking Time: 30 minutes

Ingredients:

You can substitute the vegetables with any other vegetables of your preference.
1 red pepper
1 yellow pepper
1 green pepper
2 red onions
1 courgette
300g mushrooms
2 garlic cloves, crushed
2 tbsps. soy sauce
2cm fresh ginger, peeled and grated
Bunch of fresh coriander
1 stalk lemongrass, chopped
4 tbsps. oil

Method:

1. Pre-heat your oven to 200°C. Oil a large baking tray and set to one side.
2. Chop all vegetables into large chunks and put to one side.
3. In a separate bowl, mix together the garlic, soy sauce, ginger, coriander, lemongrass, and oil. Mix well until combined.
4. Pour in your vegetables, mix together until all vegetables are coated in the seasoning.
5. Pour onto the baking tray and bake in the oven for around 30 minutes. Checking frequently and mixing around on the baking tray.
6. Once all the vegetables are soft and cooked, you can serve immediately.

Zimbabwean Peanut Butter Rice

Servings: 4
Prep Time: 5 Minutes
Cook Time: 25-30 Minutes

Ingredients:

250g rice (long grain or basmati, whichever you prefer)
1 level tbsp peanut butter
pinch of salt
pinch of sugar (preferably brown sugar)
water

Method:

1. Wash the rice thoroughly by washing it in warm water, continuously draining it until the water runs clear.
2. Put the rice in a saucepan, and cover with boiling water. Add the salt.
3. Bring the rice to the boil, once boiling turn the heat down to medium, let it simmer for 5 minutes. Turn the heat off, put a lid on the pan, and let the heat steam the rice.
4. After 15 to 20 minutes, you should have fluffy cooked rice.
5. Add in the peanut butter and mix it through.
6. Add the sugar and turn the heat back to a low heat. Cook for 5 minutes, whilst stirring. If you feel it burning at the bottom, you can add a little bit more water.
7. Now add 1 level tbsp of peanut butter and mix the rice thoroughly.

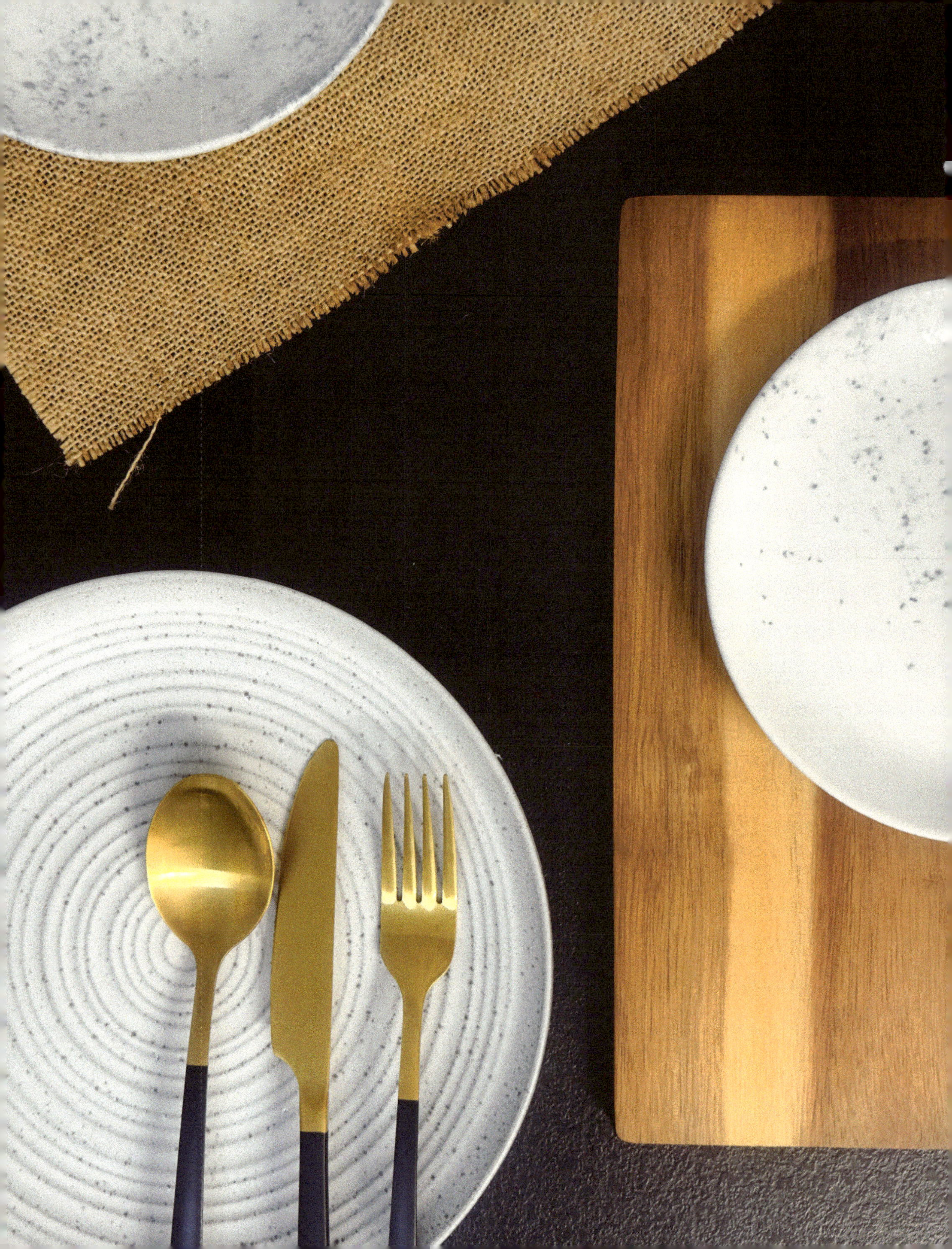

Desserts

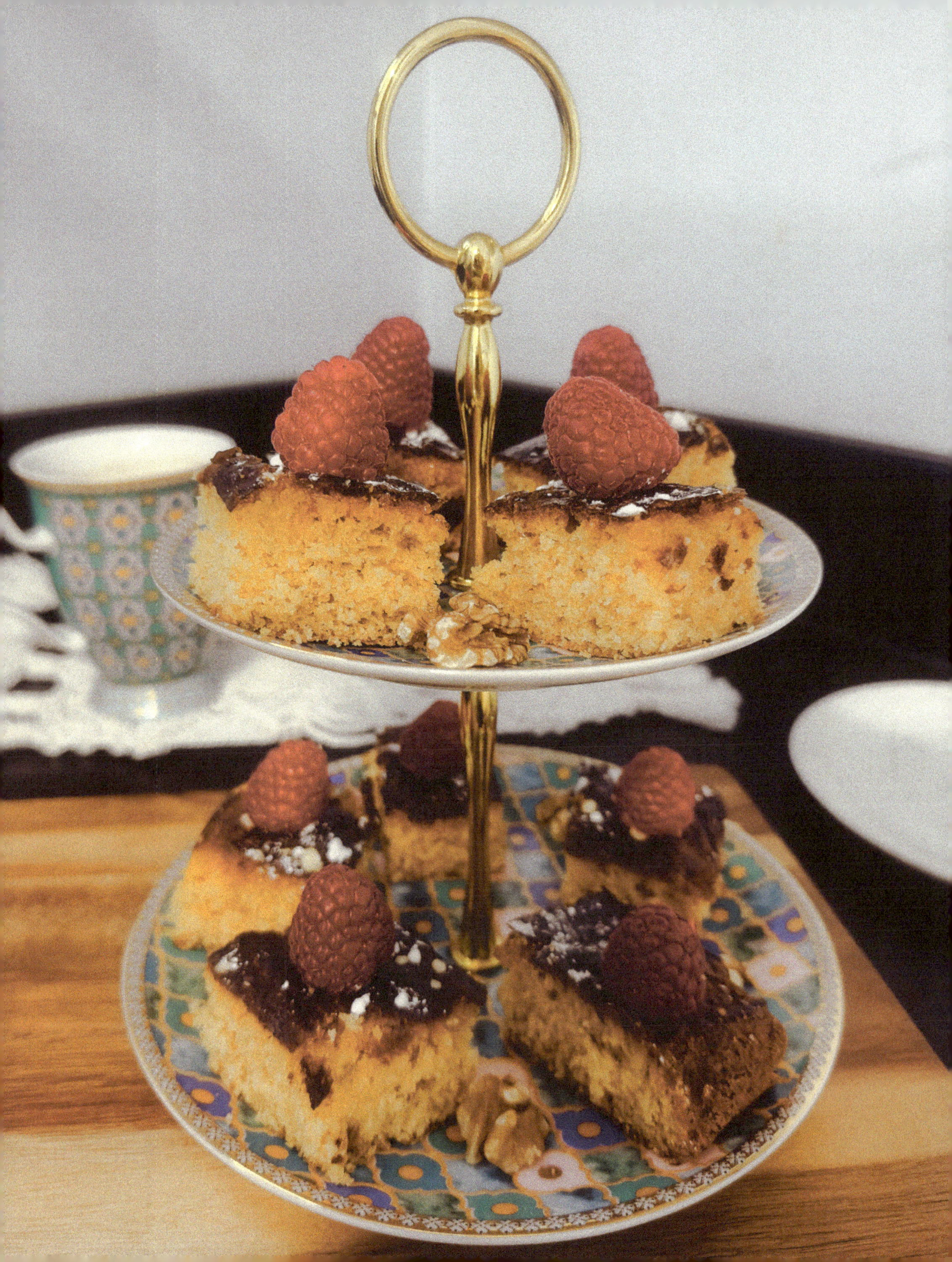

Albanian Shendetlihje – Honey and Walnut Syrup Cake

Shendetlihje (shun-det-lea)
Servings: 6 to 8

Prep Time: 15 minutes
Cooking Time: 30 minutes
Syrup Cooking Time: 20 minutes

Ingredients:
3 Eggs
200g butter
100g sugar
150g honey
1 ½ cups of flour
1 tbsp baking powder
handful of crushed walnuts

For the syrup
500ml Water
500g sugar
½ lemon juice
1 tsp of vanilla essence

Method:

1. Separate a yolk from one of the eggs and put it aside. You will need it later on. Use the rest of the eggs in step 2.
2. Add the eggs, sugar, butter, honey and nuts into a bowl and whisk together until the sugar has dissolved. You can use a machine or do this by hand.
3. Once mixed, gradually add the flour and baking powder. Do this in stages, until you get a dough like mixture.
4. Put baking paper on a baking tray and spread the mixture out to the thickness of roughly 3 cm.
5. Brush the yolk you previously saved on top of the mixture. This is important as it prevents the mixture from drying out in the oven.
6. Heat the oven to 180°C. This only needs to be pre heated for 5 minutes or so as the oven does not need to be really hot.
7. Bake the mixture in the oven for 25 to 30 minutes.
8. The syrup will soften the mixture, so do not panic if the mixture comes out quite hard after cooking.

9. Use a clean toothpick or knife to see if the mixture is cooked. Poke the toothpick in, if it comes out clean, this mixture is done. If not, put it back in for an extra 5 minutes, and repeat until the toothpick is clean.
10. Once the mixture is cooked, take it out of the oven and put it aside. Wait for it to cool down.
11. Once the cake is cool, you can begin the syrup. Timing is key here, as the cake needs to be cool, but the syrup warm. So do not start the syrup until the cake is cool and ready.
12. In a saucepan add the water and sugar. Let them boil on a medium heat for roughly 10 minutes without a lid. You do not want the syrup too thick, so continuously watch it.
13. Once the syrup has boiled for 10 minutes, turn the heat off and leave it to cool down for 5 minutes. It is important to not allow the syrup to cool down too much. It needs to be the perfect temperature. It needs to cool for exactly 5 minutes, so please set a timer.
14. After 5 minutes, add the lemon juice and vanilla extract to the syrup.
15. Slowly pour the syrup onto the baked cake.
16. Straight after pouring the syrup, cover the baking tray with foil. You want the heat of the syrup kept in the cake for 10 minutes.
17. After 10 minutes, you can serve the cake on a plate. You can add fresh fruit to decorate and serve with ice cream.

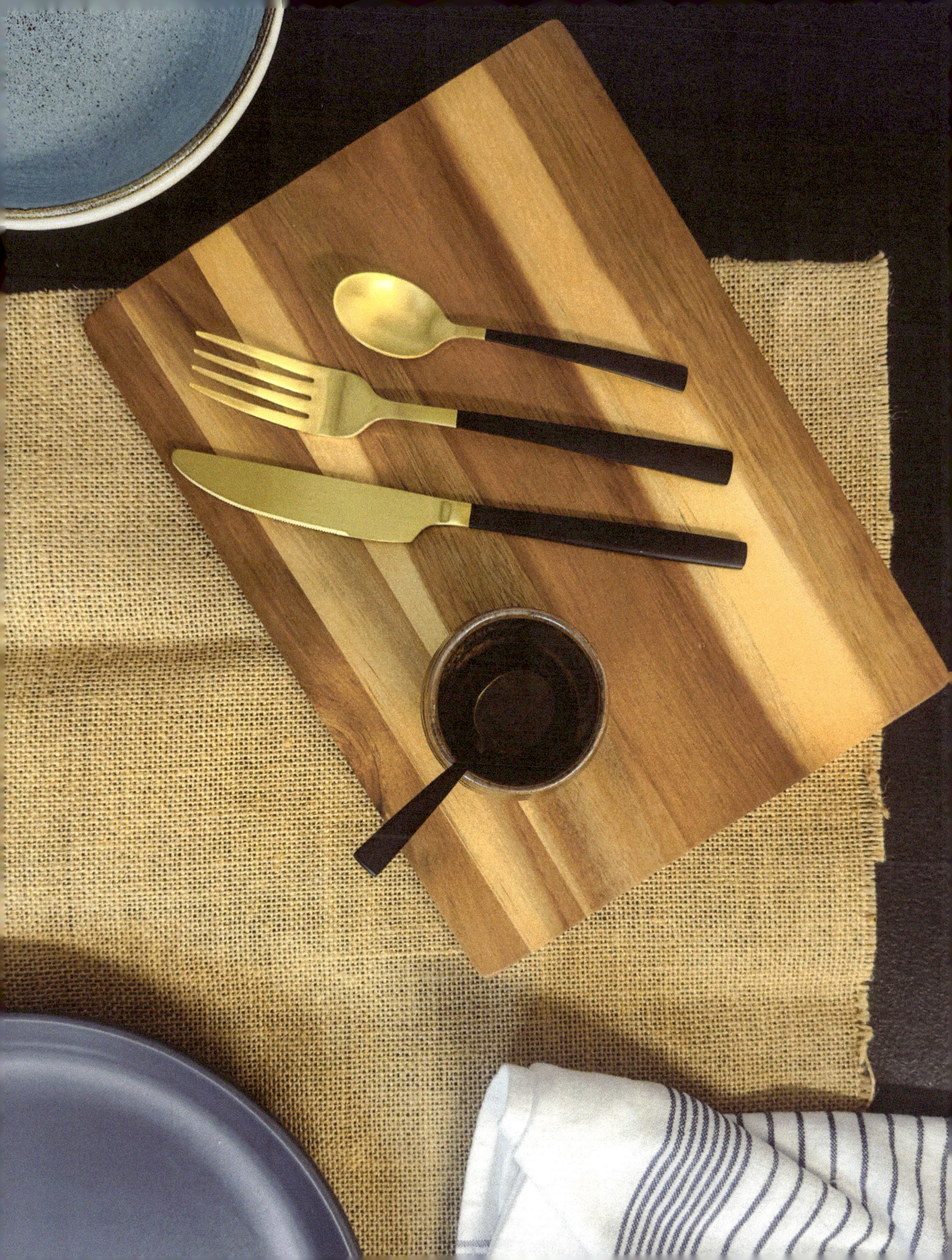

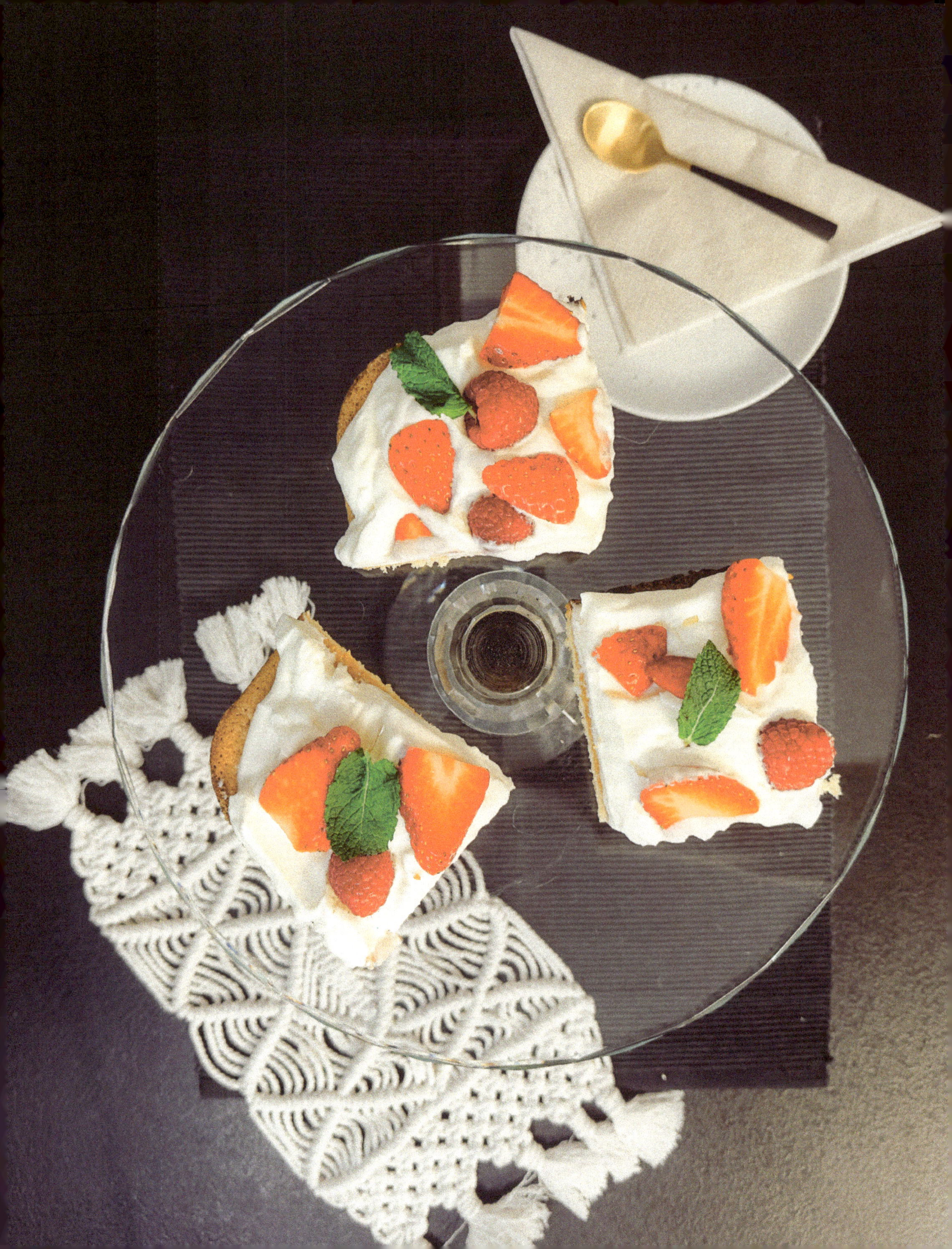

Albanian Tres Leches – Milk Sponge Cake

Servings: 8
Prep Time: 12 min
Cooking Time: 25 min

Ingredients:
120g self-raising flour
110g caster sugar
2 tsps. vanilla essence
4x eggs
pinch of salt
410g evaporated milk
200ml sweetened condensed milk
300ml double cream
2 tbsps. icing sugar
fresh fruit of your choice to decorate. We advise strawberries and raspberries.

Method:

1. Preheat your oven to 180°C.
2. Separate the egg whites from the yolks and keep them in separate bowls.
3. Add the sugar and vanilla essence to the yolks. Beat together until the mixture turns white.
4. In the separate bowl, beat the egg whites with a pinch of salt.
5. Combine the two mixtures together with smooth movements.
6. Gradually sift the flour into the mixture. Stir gently to obtain a nice and fluffy dough.
7. Grease a cake tin with a diameter of 22 cm and pour in the sponge cake dough.
8. Bake the mixture in the oven for 20 to 25 minutes.
9. When the sponge cake is ready, remove it from the oven. Put it to one side and leave to cool for 10 minutes.
10. In the meantime, mix together the evaporated milk, condensed milk, and 3 tablespoons of cream.
11. After the cake has cooled for 10 minutes, use a toothpick or skewer, to poke holes in the cake. Pour over half of the milk mixture. After 5 minutes, most of it should have soaked into the cake. Leave for another 5 minutes, and then transfer to another plate. Gradually pour over the remaining milk mixture. If it looks like it'll overflow, stop. You can serve any excess mixture with the cake.
12. In a bowl, whip together the remaining cream and icing sugar. Whisk until you have a spreadable consistency.
13. Spread the cream on top of the cake and top with fresh fruit of your choice.

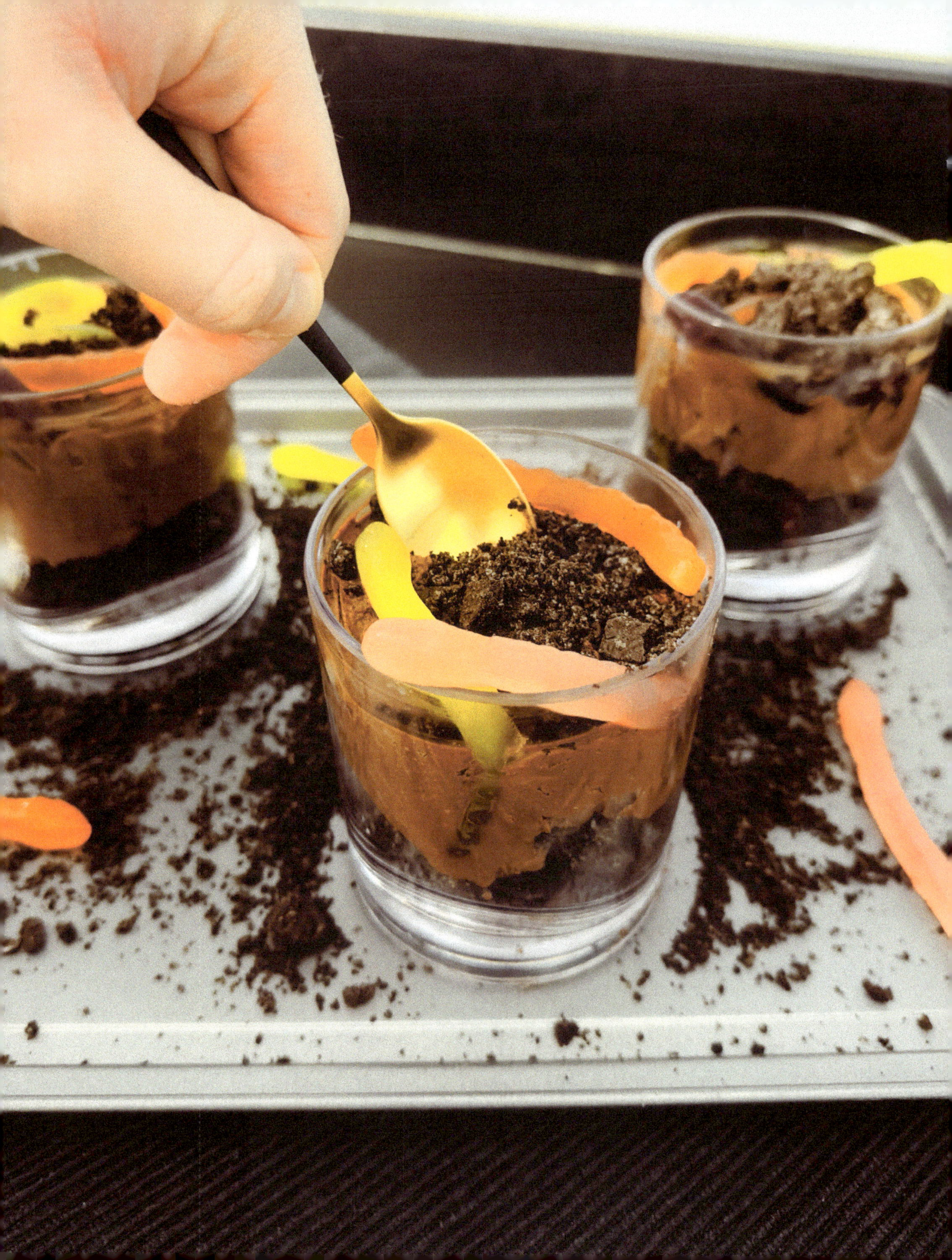

American Worms in Mud Dessert – Chocolate and Oreo Cheesecakes

Servings: 6
Prep Time: 30 minutes

Ingredients:

plastic clear cups
1x packet cream-filled sandwich cookies – such as Oreos.
1 x packet of gummy worms candy
150g dark chocolate
120ml double cream
2 tsp cocoa powder
200g full-fat cream cheese
115g caster sugar

Method:

1. Place cookies into a resealable plastic bag and crush with a rolling pin into crumbs. Put to one side.
2. Put the chocolate in a microwavable bowl. Melt the chocolate in short bursts in the microwave. Leave it to cool slightly.
3. In a separate bowl, whip the cream until soft peaks form.
4. Then fold in the cocoa powder.
5. In a separate bowl, beat the cream cheese and sugar together.
6. Fold the cocoa and cream mixture together. Once mixed, add the melted chocolate and mix well together.
7. Sprinkle some of the crushed mixture into the bottom of each plastic cup. Ensuring you leave 1/3 of the cookie crumbs left for the tops.
8. On top of the crush cookies, add a layer of the chocolate mixture. Spread evenly between all cups.
9. Smooth out the top of the pudding, then top with the rest of the chocolate cookie crumbs to resemble dirt.
10. Poke gummy worms halfway into the dirt. Refrigerate until serving.

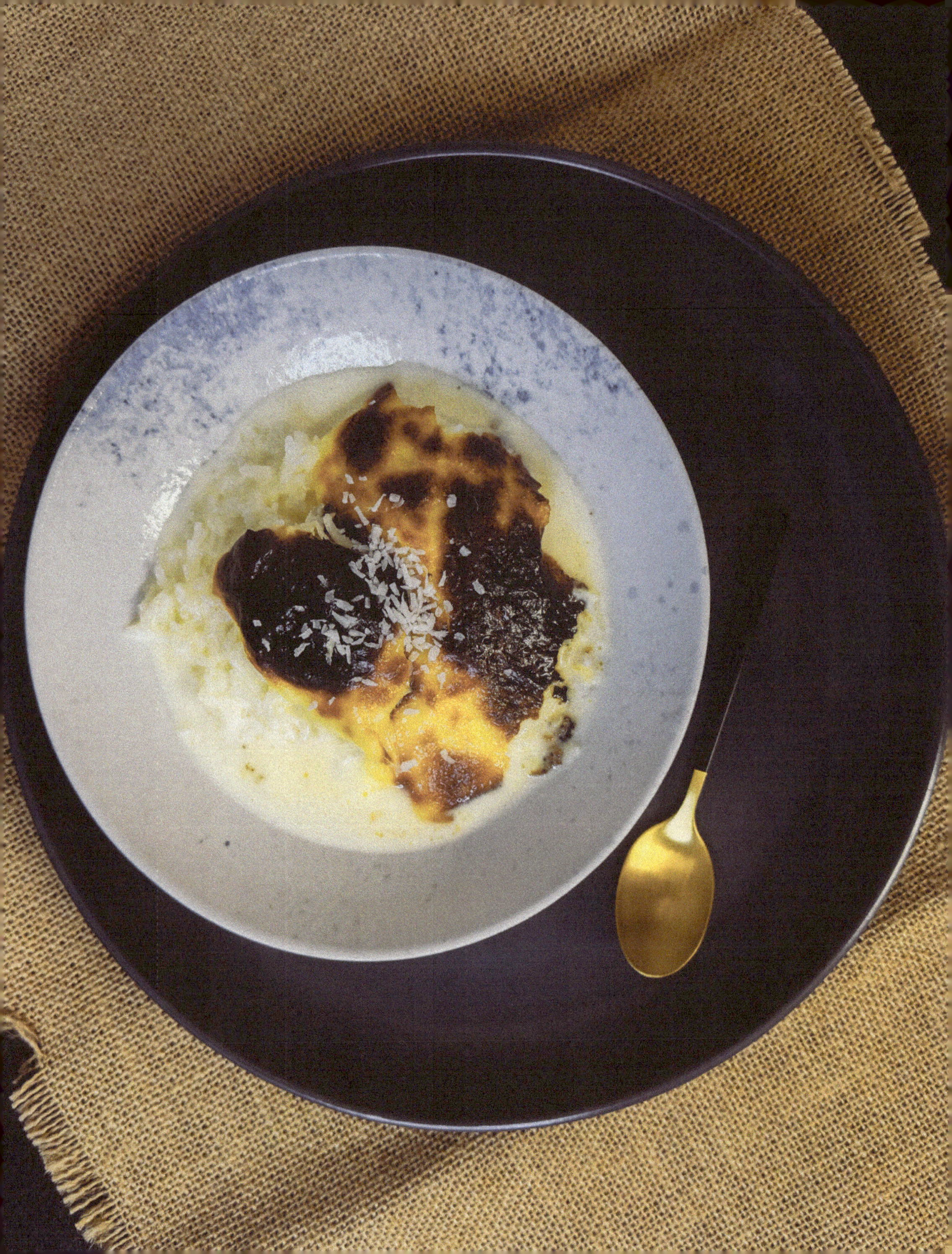

Brazilian Sweet Rice – Coconut and Cinnamon Rice Pudding

Servings: 8
Prep Time: 10 minutes
Cooking Time: 30 minutes

Ingredients

240g rice
120g sugar
1 litre water
600ml double cream
400g condensed milk
500ml milk
200g grated coconut
1 tbsp ground cinnamon

Method:

1. Pre-heat your oven to 200°C.
2. Add the rice and water to pan, bring to the boil, and let it simmer on a low heat. Boil until the rice is soft and cooked.
3. Once the water reduces, add the sugar. It's important not to let the water reduce completely.
4. Add the cream, condensed milk, and coconut. Mix everything together until it is all combined.
5. Then pour all the milk into the mixture.
6. Put the mixture into an oven proof dish, sprinkle over the cinnamon.
7. Bake in the oven for 20 minutes.
8. Serve and enjoy straight away!

Sponsors

This book would not have been possible without the generous support of our three exceptional sponsors. These organisations provided the necessary funding for its creation and publication. Through their contributions, they have championed and supported survivors at The Liberty Project and around the world.

Headline Sponsor:

THE COMPLEAT FOOD GROUP

A food group on a mission to create great quality, tasty, and affordable food, that people love to eat.

The River Foundation

Riversfoundation.co.uk

A Foundation with the aim of providing support for children and young adults.

Shell Bay Restaurant

Shellbay.net

A seafood restaurant in Dorset.

Thank You

We are incredibly grateful for the generous support of several outstanding professionals who contributed to this book pro bono. Their passion for helping survivors and their willingness to share their exceptional skills have been invaluable. By dedicating their free time, they have not only created a beautiful book but also advocated for survivors everywhere. This project would not have been possible without their dedication and expertise. Thank you from the bottom of our hearts—you are all inspiring and driving meaningful change.

Book Cover by: Aidan Saunders Graphic Design – www.aidansaundersdesign.com

An experienced freelance graphic designer offering an exceptional service. Providing bespoke illustrations for companies and individuals.

Aidan can also be found on Instagram @aidansaundersdesign

Photos by: Emna Naji - @emnafrances.art

Photo Retouching by: Ben Ingram - @framesbyben

Please check out Emna and Ben on Instagram to see more of their amazing work. Both are incredibly talented individuals offering creative services in the Dorset area.

BCHA

We are a charitable housing association supporting individuals and families across the South West and South of England. We are a major provider of a diverse range of housing, support and learning services for socially excluded people.

We have a continuing mission to meet housing need and end homelessness. We aim to achieve this through the building and provision of affordable and secure homes, and by supporting individuals to take control and lead independent, fulfilled lives.

Whether we are developing sites or supporting people with housing or learning, we believe in equality, the importance of every individual and the right to be valued and treated with dignity and respect. Our doors are open to everyone.

We manage over 1300 properties and support thousands of individuals each year.

Our work spans:
- HOME: Providing homes at social and affordable rents
- SUPPORT: Supporting individuals at risk of homelessness
- LEARN: Supporting people to turn their lives around and achieve their ambitions
- ENTERPRISE: Collaborating with our communities to create value add entrepreneurial solutions

Our Vision

Everyone has a home and the opportunity to thrive.

Our Mission

To help people take control of their own lives and find a way forward. We collaborate with others to provide this, whilst we focus on homes, wellbeing and learning.

www.bcha.org.uk

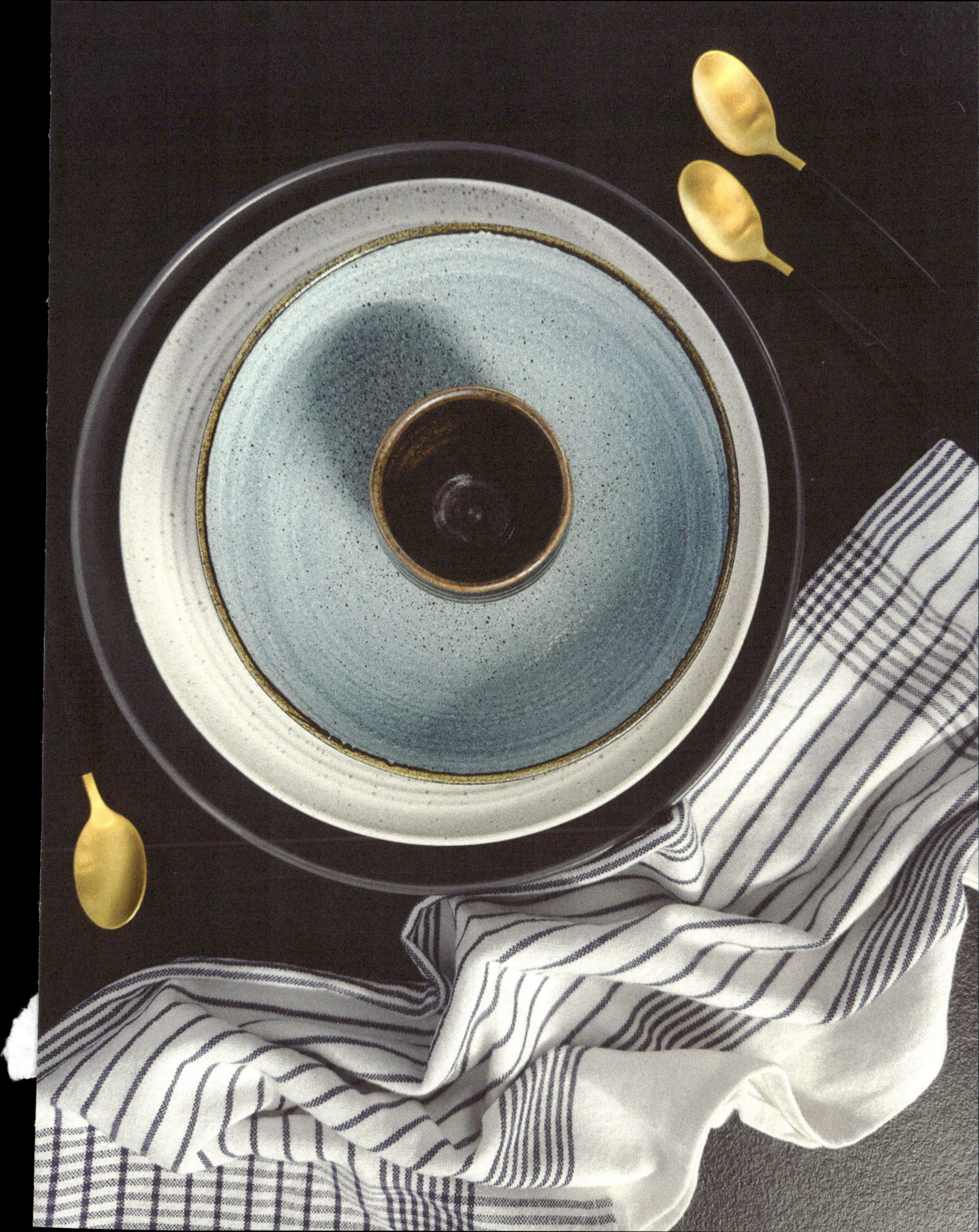